RACES AND PEOPLE

Races and People

William C. Boyd, Ph.D.
and
Isaac Asimov, Ph.D.

Illustrated by
John Bradford

Abelard-Schuman, New York

© Copyright 1955
by Isaac Asimov and William C. Boyd

Library of Congress
Catalog Card Number: 55-8630

Printed in the United States of America

Published simultaneously in Canada
by Nelson, Foster & Scott, Ltd.

To

LYLE AND GERTRUDE

Contents

CHAPTER		PAGE
1	THE MYSTIC WORD "RACE"	11
	People Are Different	11
	People Identify	12
	Racism	15
	Species and Race	18
	The Confusions of Race	22
2	WHAT RACES ARE NOT	25
	National Characteristics	25
	National Purity	28
	Languages and Nationalism	30
	Language Families	33
	Are Languages the Answer?	37
3	SKIN AND BONES	41
	The Cultural vs. the Physical	41
	Skin	43
	Hair	47
	Eyes	49
	Bones	50
	Heads	51
	Are Physical Differences the Answer?	54
4	THROUGH THE MICROSCOPE	58
	Drops of Life	58
	How Cells Divide	62
	Inside the Chromosome	65
	Enzymes and Genes	69
	Genes and Physical Characteristics	71
5	FROM PARENT TO CHILD	74
	The Egg Cell and the Sperm Cell	74

CHAPTER		PAGE
	Two Half-Cells Make a Whole Cell	77
	Male and Female	81
	Variations among the Genes	84
6	THE RULES OF INHERITANCE	94
	Mendel and His Peas	94
	The Odds of Three to One	97
	The Disadvantage of Small Numbers	99
	Genes in the Plural	101
	The Y-Chromosome Again	104
7	RULES CAN BE BROKEN	110
	Locating the Gene	110
	The Outside Influences	113
	The Sudden Change	115
	Changes for the Worse	118
	Changes for the Better	120
8	THE TELLTALE BLOOD	125
	Race, by Way of Genes	125
	The Differences in Blood	126
	The Blood Groups A, B, and O	132
	Solomon's Judgment	136
	Other Blood Groups	142
9	RACES AT LAST	145
	The Advantages of Blood Groups	145
	The Key Word: Frequency	146
	Mapping the World by Genes	149
	Human History by Genes	151
	The Human Races, by Genes	155
10	THE PRESENT AND FUTURE OF RACE	162
	What About Racism?	162
	What About the Future?	168
	The Improvement of Man	171
INDEX		177

Illustrations

	PAGE
Map of imaginary trip from Genoa to the Sudan	23
Map showing races of Europe on the basis of language	35
Map showing races of the world on the basis of skin color	44
Head shapes	52
Map showing races of Europe, North Africa, and the Middle East, on the basis of head shapes	53
Cells	61
How Cells Divide	63
How New Chromosomes Are Formed	68
Male and Female Sex Cells	75
Mitosis and Maturation	78
How Chromosomes Split Up and Re-unite	80
The Decision: Male or Female	83
How a Recessive Gene Seems to Disappear	87
How a Recessive Gene Reappears	92
Sex-Linked Inheritance, Case 1	106

	PAGE
Sex-Linked Inheritance, Case 2	107
Crossing-Over	111
Mutation	117
Transfusions, Life-Saving and Deadly	129
Blood of Various Types	131
Agglutination	133
Parentage, Possible and Impossible, Case 1	137
Parentage, Possible and Impossible, Case 2	139
Parentage, Possible and Impossible, Case 3	141
Map showing amounts of blood group gene B in the populations of the Eastern hemisphere	150
Map showing major races of the world, on the basis of inherited characteristics	159

1

The Mystic Word "Race"

PEOPLE ARE DIFFERENT

NO TWO HUMAN BEINGS look exactly alike. A child learns that fact very early in life. He can tell the difference between his mother and other women before he can talk. When he is old enough to run about, he has no trouble in recognizing his various playmates and telling them apart.

This is not at all surprising. Think of the many ways in which just a part of us—the head for example—can vary. Hair can be long or short, bushy or thinning, or not there at all. It can be wavy, curly, or straight; black, brown, red, gray, blond, white, or combinations of those shades. Complexions can be dark, fair, or medium. Eyes can be blue, brown, or something in between. Mouths can be large or small, and lips can be full or narrow. Chins can be prominent or not; noses can be straight, hooked, or snub; ears can be set at various angles. The list of differences is practically endless.

As a child grows older and observes the people about him more closely, he probably begins to notice something else, even if nobody points it out to him. Certain types of features and characteristics often occur together. For instance, people with very fair skin usually have blue eyes and blond hair. They are likely to have high-bridged noses and thin lips. On the other hand, people with dark complexions probably have dark eyes and dark hair, too. People with very dark skins often have hair that is short and kinky. Their noses are usually broad and low-bridged and their lips thick.

Later, this child we are speaking of may make still another observation. He may notice that particular types of features often run in families. In some families, blond hair and blue eyes occur quite often. In other families, black hair and brown eyes may be the rule. He may observe that a child of tall parents is more likely to grow tall than a child of short parents.

In this way, even with no one to tell him so, a child may decide that the human beings in the world can be divided into different groups. The members of each are in some way more closely related to one another than to outsiders. For that reason they resemble one another more than they resemble outsiders. Such a group of human beings is called a *race*.

PEOPLE IDENTIFY

From what we have said up to now, the idea of race would seem to have nothing wrong or dangerous about it. Yet the notion of race has given rise to much unhappiness, to cruelty and suffering, to wars and death.

Why? Well, to begin with, people *identify*. That is, they look upon themselves as belonging to a certain group. All the accomplishments of the group as a whole can then be looked upon as the individual's own accomplishments, and he can glory in them.

For instance, a boy may quarrel with another boy and say, "My big brother can lick your big brother." The boy may not be at all confident that he himself can lick the other boy. Still, as long as he can tell himself that his brother can lick the other boy's brother, he himself has gained something, and he feels more important to himself.

In the same way, children will form gangs and be convinced that "my gang can lick your gang." Older boys, and men, too, will become fans of a particular baseball team. The team's victories will become great events for them, and the defeats will be real tragedies.

It is very tempting to believe that the group with which you identify yourself is better than similar groups. Your family is better than the neighbor's family; your gang is better than the gang on the next street; your town's baseball team is better than the next town's.

Belief in superiority and inferiority is hard to shake. In baseball, for example, the rivalry between the New York Giants and the Brooklyn Dodgers is well known. Giant fans and Dodger fans will argue violently about the merits of their teams all season long. Neither group is ever persuaded by the arguments. The Giants may finish higher in the standings one year, the Dodgers in another; but that makes no difference. The arguments go on.

Like most identifications, this is a matter of emotion, rather than of reason.

Rivalries of this sort rarely reach a danger-point. You may hear about families "feuding" to the death in some parts of the country, or about juvenile gangs fighting with knives, or even of a Dodger fan shooting a Giant fan, but all this is exceptional.

Some identifications, however, are more serious. For instance, you speak English, and almost everyone you know speaks English. You might not be aware that you identify yourself with other English-speaking people; but, if you were suddenly to meet an individual who spoke only (to take an example) Bulgarian, he would seem strange to you for that reason alone. He would be a "foreigner." You might find his manner of speech interesting or amusing, or you might dislike it and find yourself suspicious of the man. You would almost certainly not be indifferent.

People are generally suspicious of any person who is different from the general population. A man with a strange language, or a type of feature that is uncommon in the surrounding group, or an odd way of dressing, or a different religion, or unusual habits of life, is felt to belong to another group of people. He is not one of your "own kind."

It does not have to be a big difference. Any of us might feel uneasy in the presence of a man wearing a turban and long, flowing garments, especially if he wore a large brass ring through his nose in addition; a man might be dressed in clothes like your own father's; yet if he frequently bowed from his waist, clicking his heels as he did so, and kissed a lady's hand when he was introduced to her, that would be enough to make you think "foreigner" at once.

When a number of people live scattered among or

surrounded by a larger group of people who differ in language, religion, social custom, or physical characteristics, the smaller group forms a *minority*. The general population often think of the minority as being apart from the group with which the majority identify themselves. Naturally, since the minority are different, it is easy to think of them as inferior. (That's the "my gang is better than your gang" psychology.) The minority may be forced to live in the more undesirable sections of a city because the better sections are closed to them. They may find it more difficult to get jobs. In general, they are discriminated against.

When people discriminate against a certain individual simply because he belongs to a minority, they are displaying *prejudice*. In our own country, the serious results of prejudice can be shown in the fact that, before 1865, many Americans thought it was quite reasonable to make slaves out of Negroes because the Negroes appeared to be different from white men. Others disagreed with this, and this disagreement was one of the causes of the long and tragic Civil War. Sadly enough, in most of the country, Negroes, although no longer slaves, are still treated with less consideration than are white men. In some regions the prejudice against them is, unfortunately, quite strong.

RACISM

It is possible for people to change their language and habits to those of the surrounding group. We have seen this happen on a large scale in America. Immigrants have reached our shores from many countries, and they or their children have learned to speak English and have become typical Americans in their ways of thinking and acting.

Some people, however, seem to think that such changes in ways and habits of living are unimportant. They assume that different groups of people develop different ways of life because of inborn differences in mind and body. Each different way of life would represent a different "race."

The German National Socialists (more commonly called Nazis), who controlled Germany from 1933 to 1945, believed this. They thought that the people of northwestern Europe, and particularly the people of Germany, had inborn qualities that made them a race apart from the rest of humanity. What's more, they thought those qualities made them a particularly superior race. The Nazis called themselves the "Herrenvolk," which is German for "master race."

The Nazis considered other groups, such as the people of Poland and Russia, to be inferior. They were especially prejudiced against the Jews of Germany. The Jews resembled other Germans in almost all respects. Many of them played important parts in German life. Some were famous scientists, important businessmen, and so on. Their chief difference from other Germans was that they were different in religion. Sometimes it was not even that, but only that their parents or grandparents had been different in this way.

Since the Nazis considered the distinction between themselves and others to be inborn, or racial, an "inferior" person was "inferior" for life. He was thought to inherit this "inferiority." Even if a man was Christian in religion, if he spoke only the best German and no other language, if he was a university professor, or an officer in the German army who had been decorated for bravery, he was still considered inferior if he had one Jewish grandparent. The Nazis acted on this theory with great cruelty and brutality, and it was partly responsible for the long and terrible World War II.

A belief that mankind may be divided not merely into races but into superior races and inferior races is known as *racism*. Naturally, if you believe your neighbor to be inferior to yourself not just because he likes spaghetti and you like hot dogs, but because he was born inferior, you are less likely to make allowances for him. You are less likely to try spaghetti yourself and see if you like it, too. You are less likely to try to introduce him to hot dogs. You are less likely to become friends as you get to know him better.

If a supposedly inferior group exists as a minority within a country, racism can result in cruelties such as those visited on the Jews in Nazi Germany, or, as we have said, on Negroes in our own country. A nation under the influence of racist thinking is more easily led to war against the "inferior" nations at its side, is likely to fight the war with greater brutality, and is more apt, if victorious, to exact a harsh peace.

It is therefore of the greatest importance to learn all we can about the races of mankind in order to see what really makes a human race and in what ways the various races are really different. It is particularly important for us of the United States now, since we, through the United Nations, are leading a large part of the world in search of peace, freedom, and security. We must not forget that many of the people we are hoping to lead differ from us widely in appearance and ways of life. If we have false notions as to what these differences mean, we may fail in our leadership.

SPECIES AND RACE

Perhaps we can get a good start if we ask: How do scientists go about classifying animals and plants? Their methods may give us hints concerning the classification of mankind.

The science of classifying living things is known as *taxonomy*. The method of taxonomy is to divide all living things into a few very broad groups on the basis of certain similarities within the groups, then to divide these groups into a number of less broad groups, then to divide these sub-groups, and so on, again and again. Each new sub-group includes fewer kinds of living organisms. As the number of kinds decreases, however, the resemblance among them increases. Finally, a sub-group is reached which includes only one kind of living organism.

All life is thus divided into two *kingdoms*: plants and animals. The animal kingdom is divided into a number of smaller groups called *phyla* (singular, *phylum*). One of these phyla, the Chordata, includes all animals that have an internal skeleton of either bone or cartilage. Examples of animals that belong among the Chordata (the chordates) are: sharks, snakes, eels, and eagles. They all have internal skeletons. Examples of animals that are *not* members of the Chordata are: snails, bees, crabs, squids, and worms. They and others like them have either external skeletons or no skeletons at all.

Each phylum is broken down into smaller groups called *classes*. One class of chordates is the *Mammalia*. This class includes all chordates which have hair, give birth to their young alive (that is, not in eggs that have to be hatched), and suckle their young on milk. Included among the Mammalia (the mammals) are: weasels, whales, cattle, monkeys, and bats. Chordates that are *not* members of the Mammalia are: fish, frogs, reptiles, and birds.

Each class is broken down into still smaller groups called *orders*. One order of mammals is the Carnivora. This order includes animals that are flesh-eating and that are related in some other ways as well. Examples of carnivores are: lions, wolves, cats, and dogs. Examples of mammals that are *not* carnivores are: sheep, deer, and rabbits.

The orders are divided into smaller groups called *families*, such as the Canidae. This family includes dogs, wolves, jackals, and foxes (but *not* lions or tigers). Families are divided into *genera* (singular, *genus*), such as Canis, which includes dogs, wolves, and some jackals, but not foxes. Finally, the genera are divided into *species*.

The species is the smallest important group in the classification and is usually considered to consist of only one kind of animal. Every creature has a Latin name of two words, the first giving the genus and the second the species. The dog is called *Canis familiaris*, and one kind of wolf is called *Canis lupus*. They belong to the same genus but to different species. Similarly, the ordinary house cat is *Felis domestica,* the lion is *Felis leo,* and the tiger is *Felis tigris.* These are different species of the same genus, and the genus is different from that which includes dogs and wolves.

Yet here comes a problem. A police dog looks much more like a wolf than it does like a Scotch terrier. Why, then, is a police dog of a different species from the wolf and of the same species as a Scotch terrier?

This brings up the whole question of how one defines a species. Such a definition is not easy, but it is usually considered that creatures belong to the same species if they interbreed freely and then give birth to fertile young. (Horses and donkeys can interbreed, but the young of such a union, called mules, are not fertile; that is, they cannot breed and bear young themselves. Horses and donkeys are therefore of different species.)

Dogs and wolves do not interbreed freely and hence are of different species. Different kinds of dogs do interbreed freely if the difference in size is not too great and if they are not prevented by human interference. The differences among the various kinds of dogs are mostly the result of *selective breeding* under human supervision. Dog-breeders who wished to develop a dog which would specialize in rapid running would mate two dogs with especially long legs and deep chests. The offspring with the longest legs and the deepest chests would then be mated with one another. Eventually, as the dog generations passed, the greyhound would be developed.

The greyhound is still *Canis familiaris,* however, and is capable of mating with dogs which have been selectively bred into other shapes or have not been selectively bred at all. In fact, if all dogs were allowed to run about free, they would interbreed with one another, and eventually each variety would lose its specialized characteristics.

How does all this apply to mankind? Man is, of course, a member of the class Mammalia. We have hair, our children are born alive, and milk is produced by mothers for the children's nourishment. We belong to the order called *primates,* which includes such mammals as lemurs, monkeys, and apes. Within that order, mankind occupies a genus all by himself. This genus is called *Homo.* Furthermore, within that genus there is only one species, the scientific name of which is *Homo sapiens.*

All human beings, however different they may appear to be, are members of this one species. As far as we know, they can all interbreed freely, regardless of skin color or language. What we call "races" are therefore, at most, like the different varieties of dog, only varieties within a single species.

Yet there is a difference: *Homo sapiens* has never really indulged in selective breeding. Men and women have their own notions about whom to choose as partners, and when they make the choice, they don't usually think about the kind of children they will have. A fast runner is very likely to marry a girl with no running talent at all so there is little chance that a fast-running breed of human beings will develop. The result is that the varieties of mankind are less different from one another than are the varieties of dogs.

Naturally, the problem of distinguishing between human races and studying each separately is all the more difficult because of that.

THE CONFUSIONS OF RACE

You may not agree with this. You may think that some human races are quite different from one another and easy to tell apart. You may take as an example a Negro and a white man. Surely, you might say, anyone can tell the difference between the two at once.

Always? Are you sure? Let's see.

Suppose we take a little trip in imagination. Let us begin our tour by taking a ship to Genoa, in northwestern Italy. There we would find a population very similar to the white American with whom we are familiar. Many of the people are blond and have blue eyes. Others have light-brown hair and eyes. A few have dark hair and eyes. The skins are, on the whole, rather light.

Now suppose we go on an automobile or rail trip southeastward down the Italian peninsula. As we go south, the characteristics of the population change. Blond hair and blue eyes disappear, and black hair and dark eyes prevail. The tint of the skin gradually becomes darker. When we reach Sicily, the island off the southern tip of Italy, we find the people quite dark-complexioned. Still, no one would judge the Sicilians to be Negroes.

Next we shall take a ship or plane and travel from Sicily to Cairo, Egypt. The people here are not all alike, and many are descended from European immigrants,

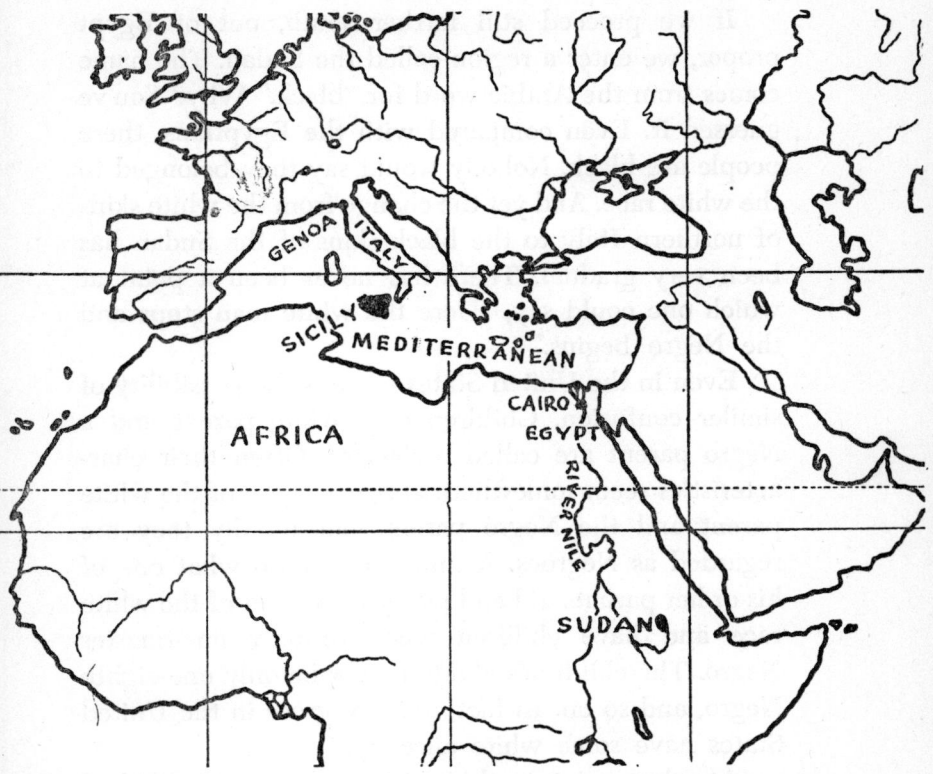

Map showing regions referred to in the journey described in text.

If we ignore the immigrants, we find that the native Egyptians are, on the whole, a little darker-skinned even than the Sicilians. Yet they are still not considered Negroes.

But wait, we can take a trip up the Nile, moving southward into the tropic zone as we do so. The skin color of the inhabitants continues to grow darker as we travel. Some of the hair is a bit kinky. Negroes or white? It begins to grow somewhat doubtful.

If we proceed still farther south, out of Egypt proper, we enter a region called the Sudan. The name comes from the Arabic word for "black." Why? You've guessed it. Even compared with the Egyptians, these people are black. Nobody would say they belonged to the white race. And yet the change from the white skins of northern Italy to the black skins of the Sudan has been very gradual. There has never been a point at which one could say, "Here the white man stops and the Negro begins."

Even in the United States there is the possibility of similar confusion. Children of a white parent and a Negro parent are called mulattoes. Often their characteristics seem somewhere between those of the white parent and the Negro parent, but usually they are regarded as Negroes. A mulatto may do what one of his or her parents did and marry a member of the white race and have children who are only one-quarter Negro. The children's children may be only one-eighth Negro, and so on. In fact, most Negroes in the United States have some white ancestry.

At what point in this mixture does an individual cease being a Negro and become a white man? Some states in the South consider that an individual is a Negro if he has any Negro ancestry at all, regardless of how little. It is therefore possible to have so little Negro heritage that all your characteristics are apparently those of a white man and yet be legally a Negro in those southern states. You might have blond hair and blue eyes and still be a Negro.

So you see the question of race is anything but a simple matter.

2

What Races Are Not

NATIONAL CHARACTERISTICS

BEFORE WE GO ON to decide what races are, let us see some of the things they are *not*. A great many people in this world have their own notions of race, and some of these notions are widespread. Unfortunately, most of them are quite wrong, too.

For instance, some people speak about "German psychology" and "French character" as though these things were something inborn, or racial. Can it be that certain national characteristics endure from generation to generation? If that were so, then the different nations would represent different races. But is it so?

Suppose we consider Germany. For the last eighty years or so, the Germans have acted very warlike. Especially during World War II, it was generally accepted by many Americans that the Germans had the greatest talent and liking for war of all the peoples on Earth. It took most of the rest of the world four years to stop them in World War I and six years to stop them in World War II. It seemed, at the time, that the Germans were just naturally cruel, ruthless, despotic. There was no way of persuading them to change, many thought, since their character was something inborn. Yet, only a few years after World War II, things don't seem quite that way any more. We are making friends with the Germans.

In comparison with the Germans, the French have seemed peace-loving and easygoing—perhaps too easygoing, too easily beaten. They were badly beaten by the Germans in 1870 and in 1940, and they were beaten again, in Indo-China, in 1954.

Yet from 1660 to 1815, a period of a hundred and fifty years, it was the French who were viewed by the rest of the world as a militaristic people with a special talent for war and with an apparent liking for it. They were forever invading their neighbors and generally disturbing the peace. Toward the end of that period, it took all of Europe not four or six, but twenty-five, years to defeat France's bid for world domination.

During that same period, Germany (except for one part of it, under Frederick the Great) seemed quite unwarlike. It was a nation famous for philosophers and musicians and was incapable of forming a political union or developing a strong government. Far from conquering its neighbors, it was at the mercy of invading armies.

About 1800, Napoleon called England "a nation of shopkeepers." In some ways that seemed true, since England at the time was mainly interested in trade and commerce rather than in military glory. For most of the period of the Napoleonic wars, England's direct military participation was rather small. For the most part she financed Austrian, Prussian, and Russian armies and let them do the fighting against France. Yet, about 1400, England was a most militaristic nation. Its armies nearly conquered France, although France outnumbered it in population by at least five to one.

Again, one could scarcely think of two more peaceful nations than Sweden and Switzerland. It seems to be their national characteristic to avoid trouble with their neighbors, to make no fusses, to get along. Neither has been at war since 1815.

Yet there was a time when Sweden was one of the most warlike nations in Europe. For the hundred years between 1630 and 1730, Swedish armies invaded, at one time or another, most of northern Europe outside its borders. Charles XII of Sweden fought Denmark, half of Germany, Poland, and Russia simultaneously for twenty years and almost won, too.

As for Switzerland, her citizens were the most feared fighters in Europe in the early sixteenth century. Swiss soldiers hired themselves out to the highest bidder as mercenaries, or paid soldiers, and various armies did their best to buy as many as possible.

To come back to our time, it was fashionable, not very long ago, to look upon Russians as melancholy peasants with beards. They might be able to write gloomy novels and turn out sad symphonies, but they could never really adapt themselves to the machine age, it seemed. Mechanical know-how just wasn't in them. I think most of us will agree that what seemed to be Russian national characteristics then don't seem to be so any longer.

In the 1930's, when Japan was trouncing the much larger China, it was common to think of the Chinese as just naturally pacifistic. They seemed a kindly, peace-loving, and long-suffering people who despised soldiers and war. On the other hand, Japan seemed a hard, aggressive, domineering nation with a special talent for hypocrisy and treachery. Again it looks as though we Americans were in the process of beginning to doubt easy decisions about national character.

There are many other examples of this sort of thing. National characteristics are *not* unchanging. For that reason, they are not something that is inherited, and they cannot, therefore, be a sign of race.

NATIONAL PURITY

Not only do national characteristics seem to be changing all the time, but all nations have mixed ancestries.

Consider first that, whenever two groups of people, who have previously been living in different regions of the world, are brought together, there is bound to be interbreeding. Children of mixed parentage are born. This takes place even when the peoples are quite different in their appearance. It takes place even when one group considers the other quite inferior.

We have already mentioned the white heritage that exists among the majority of Negroes in the United States. A similar situation holds for the Indians of the New World, to some extent in what is now the United States and Canada, and more so in Latin America. In Mexico and in many of the nations south of it, the white newcomers (mostly from Spain and Portugal) interbred with the Indians. The children of such unions interbred with one another, with Indians, with whites, with Negroes who were later brought to some parts of Latin America from Africa. The people of mixed heritage who so developed are called *mestizos*.

In some Latin American countries the majority of the population is mestizo.

Do such mixtures take place in Europe, too? Well, every country has suffered invasions, and every one of these invasions undoubtedly led to interbreeding between the invading armies and the native women. (A modern example of this can be seen in the children being born in countries such as France, Germany, Italy, and Japan, whose fathers were among the soldiers of the occupying American armies.)

Germany, for which Hitler made many claims of racial "purity" and where the Nazis worried about the danger of "contamination" with what they considered to be inferior races, is no exception. Considering fairly modern times only, Germany was invaded, between 1618 and 1815, by the enemy armies (or the allied "friendly" armies) of the following nations: Denmark, Sweden, Russia, England, Spain, and France. There are also various Balkan contingents in the Austrian armies to be considered. Each group undoubtedly left behind its "contaminating" mark, so that by Hitler's time little "purity" could have existed.

If we go farther back in time, we find whole nations or peoples migrating from the depths of Asia to Europe. Some of these remained for centuries, or even to the present day.

Let us take an example of the kind of mixing that goes on. In the seventh century Arab armies invaded North Africa, converting the Berber natives to the new Mohammedan religion. Undoubtedly, interbreeding went on. In the early eighth century an army of "Moors" (consisting mostly of Berbers, but with some

Arabs) invaded and conquered Spain. They remained in parts of Spain for nearly 800 years, and during that time there were occasional arrivals of new tribes from North Africa. Undoubtedly, the modern Spaniard has some Moorish heritage. In 1588 a Spanish fleet attempted the invasion of England. It failed, and some ships were destroyed by storms off the coast of Ireland. Some Spanish soldiers and sailors managed to reach the Irish shores alive. They remained and undoubtedly interbred in Ireland.

In the middle of the nineteenth century many Irish emigrated to the United States, where they now form a large and honored portion of our population, marrying freely with Americans of non-Irish descent. In 1945, an American army of occupation, including many persons of Irish or part-Irish descent, landed in Japan and remained for years. Again interbreeding took place.

In this way we could possibly trace an Arab heritage by way of North Africa, Spain, Ireland, and America, in children growing up in Japan now.

Of course, it must be admitted that any Arab ancestry in Japan must be so small that it might as well be ignored. Still, this is only intended as an example. Mixing such as this has been proceeding on Earth ever since history began, and the effect piles up through the centuries. It is silly to expect that any line on the map marks off a people with pure ancestry.

LANGUAGES AND NATIONALISM

When we think of the differences between two different nations, we usually think first of all of the fact that they generally speak two different languages.

(The most important exceptions are Great Britain and the United States, both of which consist of English-speaking people.)

Almost every nation in Europe speaks a language of its own. The language may, in fact, be more important than political allegiance. People with a common language have a common literature and, therefore, common traditions of many kinds. A Greek-speaking inhabitant of the island of Cyprus may feel that he has more in common with the Greek-speaking people of Greece than with the English-speaking people who rule him. When Hitler spoke of Germans, he meant not just the population of Germany, but anyone who spoke German as a native language anywhere in the world. This identification, on the part of European peoples, with a language, rather than with a political unit, is known as *nationalism*.*

Nationalism has sometimes resulted in the formation of nations. For instance, in the early nineteenth century the Italian peninsula was divided into small independent units such as Naples, Sardinia, Parma, Modena, and Tuscany. The inhabitants of all of these spoke Italian. In addition, people in parts of the Austro-Hungarian Empire, such as the provinces of Lombardy and Venetia, also spoke Italian. As a result of a series of wars in which these Italian units, led by Sardinia, took part, all were united into the Kingdom of Italy.

In similar fashion, under the leadership of Prussia,

---

* Since 1900, various peoples in Asia and Africa have also experienced nationalism. This, however, is not quite like Europe's nationalistic movements. Language is not always the most important consideration. Sometimes it is religion. Sometimes it is dislike of some European country which is in power.

a number of small states in central Europe, the subjects of which spoke German, were united into the German Empire.

On the other hand, nationalism can break up a political unit. Within the Austro-Hungarian Empire there were people who spoke various languages such as Polish, Serbian, Rumanian, Italian, and Czech. All were more or less dissatisfied to be ruled by people who spoke German. After World War I and the defeat of Austria-Hungary, these "subject peoples" formed countries of their own or joined neighboring independent peoples that spoke their language.

The problem of nationalism did not cease with World War I. A great many of the troubles that led to World War II involved German-speaking people who lived outside Germany proper, notably in Austria, Czechoslovakia, and Poland. Since World War II, nationalistic feeling has been growing in countries that are colonies or have recently been colonies—especially in North Africa, the Middle East, and Southeast Asia.

Is it possible, then, that languages are the clue by which we can divide mankind into races? Certainly, the language seems to be a more accurate indication of the ancestry of a people than is the political unit within which they happen to live.

For instance, there are German-speaking colonies throughout Europe. Before World War II they extended to points as distant from Germany as the Volga River in Russia. Half a million people on the Volga were descended from Germans brought in by Catherine the Great in the eighteenth century. Because they live on the Volga, one would suppose they were Russians if one didn't know that they retained the use of the German language.

From 1795 to 1918 there was no country named Poland on the map of Europe. Yet for nearly a thousand years before 1795 there had been a Poland. It had been divided among Prussia (which later formed the main part of Germany), Austria, and Russia and was gone as far as the map-makers were concerned. But the people of what had been Poland retained their language and their feeling of kinship with one another. When all three of the devouring empires had been defeated in World War I, a new Poland was founded.

This way languages have of hanging on even when a nation is defeated or scattered is not confined to Europe. France once owned Canada and the central third of what is now the United States. Her political rule vanished in 1763 in Canada and in 1803 in the United States. Yet a large minority of the Canadian population (mainly in the province of Quebec) still speak French, and there are traces of the French language in the state of Louisiana.

A similar case is that of the Pennsylvania "Dutch." They have lived in Pennsylvania since the youth of the nation but still speak a form of German, thus showing their German descent.

LANGUAGE FAMILIES

People who study languages find that they can be classified into groups and sub-groups. By studying similarities in vocabulary, grammar, and word order, they decided that most European languages, living and dead, and some Asiatic languages such as Persian and Sanskrit, are all descended from a single language. This group of languages is referred to as *Indo-European*.

Within this group of languages one can discover sub-groups. For instance, there is a sub-group of *Germanic* languages, such as English, Swedish, German, and Dutch. There are the *Romance* languages, such as Spanish, Portuguese, French, Italian, and Rumanian. There are the *Slavic* languages, such as Russian, Polish, Bulgarian, and Serbian. The languages in each group resemble one another more closely than they resemble languages outside the group. (There are also some European languages that belong to none of these groups and a few that are not Indo-European at all.)

This is what one might expect to find if once, in early history, some group of people speaking the original Indo-European language entered Europe and divided into three branches, one settling in eastern Europe, one in northern Europe, and one in southern Europe. Gradually, with separation and isolation, each would develop its own version of the common tongue: Slavic in the east, Germanic in the north, Romance in the south.

Each branch was further subdivided with the passage of history. Two thousand years ago the inhabitants of the territory that is now Spain, Portugal, France, and Italy (plus other regions as well) all spoke Latin. About 500 A.D. these regions were invaded and occupied by tribes from the north, speaking Germanic languages. Civilization declined, and with it education and communication. The various groups of people lost touch with one another. In separation each

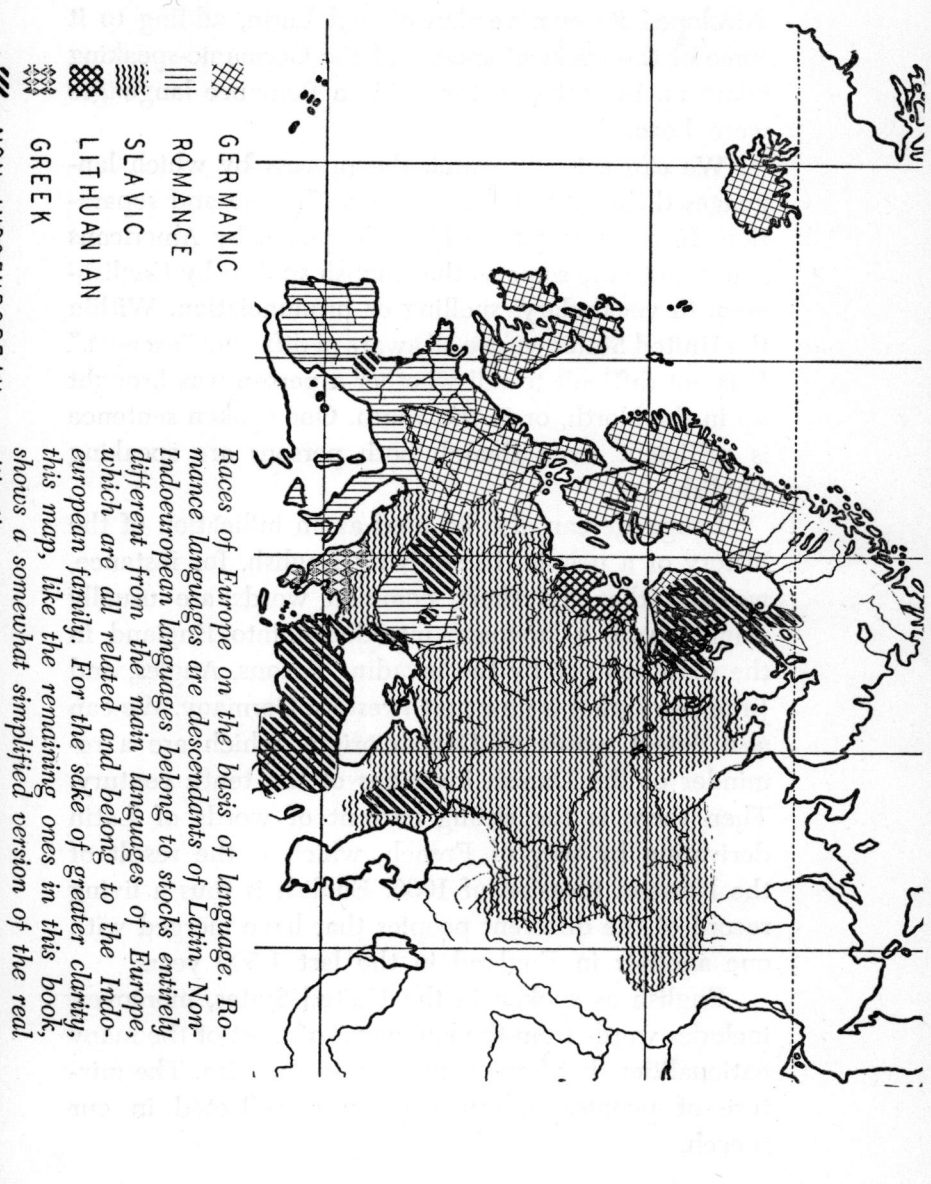

Races of Europe on the basis of language. Romance languages are descendants of Latin. Non-Indoeuropean languages belong to stocks entirely different from the main languages of Europe, which are all related and belong to the Indo-european family. For the sake of greater clarity, this map, like the remaining ones in this book, shows a somewhat simplified version of the real situation.

GERMANIC
ROMANCE
SLAVIC
LITHUANIAN
GREEK
NON-INDOEUROPEAN

developed its own version of bad Latin, adding to it some of the tricks of speech of the Germanic-speaking invaders. In that way the modern Romance languages were born.

We can actually watch the process by which languages differentiate themselves with time and separation. In many ways the English spoken by Americans is not quite the same as the English spoken by Englishmen, in vocabulary, spelling or pronunciation. Within the United States we are all aware of different "accents." It is not difficult to tell whether a person was brought up in the North, or in the South. One spoken sentence is sufficient, even though both persons are speaking English.

Language can also be used as an indication of the history of a people. In studying English, for instance, we find that the short, common words are usually Anglo-Saxon, a language introduced into England in the sixth century by the invading Saxons, Angles, and Jutes from what is now northwestern Germany. We can also detect words of Danish origin, which are a reminder of the Danish invasions of the tenth century. Then there is the strong current of words of Latin derivation by way of French, which is the result of the Norman invasion of 1066. English is thus a living record of the different peoples that have merged with one another in England in the last 1,500 years.

English as spoken in the United States, moreover, includes words from the languages of most of the many nationalities that have emigrated to America. The mixture of peoples in our country is reflected in our speech.

Outside the Indo-European family altogether are other groups of languages that resemble one another. There are the *Semitic* languages, for example, which include Arabic, Aramaic, and Hebrew. These languages are called "Semitic" because the people speaking them are described in the Bible as being descended from Noah's oldest son, Shem. Similarly, there is the group of *Hamitic* languages, including Coptic (the older language of Egypt) and some of the Ethiopian tongues. This name is derived from Noah's second son, Ham, who is described in the Bible as the ancestor of the Egyptian people.

Another group of languages spoken in Europe is the *Finno-Ugrian*. This includes the Finnish and Hungarian languages. These are more closely related to Turkish, it is thought, than to any of the languages mentioned earlier.

ARE LANGUAGES THE ANSWER?

In the nineteenth century the idea of language as the key to race became popular with some people. Certain Germans, for instance, developed a *pan-Germanism*—a belief that the peoples speaking Germanic languages were superior to all others and were destined to rule the other, "inferior" races. In Russia there was, on the other hand, a *pan-Slavism*—an attempt to achieve a union of all Slavic-speaking peoples and a belief that the Slavs were superior. (In all race theories the people developing the theory consider themselves superior. It is never the other fellow.)

Hitler's race theories were also based on language. He considered "Aryans" to be superior to other "races."

(Sometimes the Indo-European languages are called the "Aryan" languages from the name of a tribe speaking such a language which once invaded India. That is where Hitler and others who thought as he did got the word.)

To Hitler, Jews and people with Jewish ancestors were "non-Aryans" and "inferior." To be sure, an early language of the Jews was Hebrew, a Semitic tongue. (It is for that reason that prejudice against Jews is referred to as *anti-Semitism*.) However, modern European Jews speak either the language of the country in which they live or Yiddish. Yiddish is a form of German with some Hebrew words and, in eastern Europe, with Slavic words as well. In any case, Yiddish is almost entirely an Indo-European, or "Aryan," language, more closely related to German than to any other language.

On the other hand, Hitler considered the Finns and the Hungarians to be "Aryans" even though their language was definitely "non-Aryan." In fact, Hitler was even friendly with the Arabs, whose language is a purely Semitic tongue very closely related to Hebrew. But then Hitler's theories never made much sense, and the more closely they are studied, the more nonsensical they seem.

The main trouble with language as a clue to race, however, is that people often adopt the language of their masters. The Poles did not, but there are people who did.

The inhabitants of Asia Minor were ruled by Greek-speaking peoples for the first one thousand years of the Christian era, and by the end of that time Greek was spoken pretty generally throughout the region. Toward the end of the eleventh century a tribe of Turks conquered the region, and the peasants learned to speak Turkish. They are now considered Turks.

The Arabs conquered Egypt and North Africa in the seventh century. Arabic was adopted as the language of this region, and Egypt and Libya are now thought of as part of an "Arab" group of nations even though their inhabitants are not much more Arab than they were before.

Suppose we consider the "English-speaking peoples." This phrase is usually taken to mean the peoples of Great Britain, Canada, Australia, New Zealand, South Africa, and the United States. The impression that is usually made by this phrase is that of a group of nations closely related by race.

When the Anglo-Saxons first invaded England, they overcame peoples that spoke *Celtic* languages. (These are Indo-European languages which lie somewhere between the Germanic group and the Romance group.) These Celtic-speaking peoples still exist in Cornwall, Wales, and Ireland, but they have all, more or less, adopted English as a language. So Ireland is today an "English-speaking country," although its heritage is quite different from that of England.

In the United States we have people of a wide variety of ancestral background, almost all of whom, including our sixteen million Negroes, speak English.

Among the independent nations whose official tongue is English must be listed the African republic of Liberia, inhabited by Negroes. Some of these are descendants of American slaves brought back to Africa during the administration of President James Monroe. This accounts for the English and for the fact that the Liberian capital is called Monrovia.

Similarly, among the "French-speaking peoples" are not only the people of France itself, plus those of southern Belgium, western Switzerland, Quebec, and parts of Louisiana, but also those of the Negro republic of Haiti in the West Indies, which was once a French colony. There are, moreover, eighteen Spanish-speaking nations and one Portuguese-speaking nation in the Western Hemisphere, with various admixtures of Negro and Indian heritage. A large number of the people of the Philippine Islands, who are related to the people of Southeast Asia, are also Spanish-speaking.

Language is therefore too easily changed to be a reliable indication of race and can, in fact, give rise to notions that are quite wrong.

3

Skin and Bones

THE CULTURAL VS. THE PHYSICAL

LANGUAGE MUST BE LEARNED. A child of French-speaking parents, living in France, is not born able to speak French. Before the child has reached the age of five, however, he will have learned to chatter French with great ease. A child of German-speaking parents living in Germany will have learned to speak German just as easily.

This is not because either child was born with any special talent for the language of his parents. If the French and German babies were exchanged in infancy, little Pierre would learn to say *"Auf Wiedersehen"* and little Hans would learn to say *"Au revoir"* just as quickly as the other way round. In fact, if little Pierre and little Hans were both brought to America in infancy and raised with American children, they would both learn to say "So long" without an accent.

Any normal infant will learn any language spoken by the people around him, no matter what the original language of his parents was.

As you can see, this in itself spoils language as an indication of race. If you close your eyes and listen to a voice speaking perfect English, you cannot know for certain whether the parents of the man owning the voice were born in New York, Shanghai, or Timbuctoo. You can't tell, just by listening to a man talk, the color of his hair, the shape of his head, or the height of his body.

The same reasoning applies to the kind of food a person likes to eat and the type of clothes he prefers to wear. Such things depend on what he grew accustomed to as he grew up. American children of immigrant parents learn to like frankfurters, hamburgers, and baked beans as easily as American children of native parents.

Differences between people which are the result of training are called *cultural differences*. Cultural differences cannot be used to divide human beings into races. That would be like trying to divide dogs into different breeds according to the tricks they could do. Imagine deciding that all dogs who could "play dead" belonged to one breed and all who could "sit up and beg" belonged to another.

What we must do, then, is make use of human characteristics which are not the result of training. We must find characteristics with which each human being is born or which develop as a man grows without his being able to do anything about it. For instance, a child is born with ten fingers and ten toes. Before very long his hair and eyes have assumed some definite color. By the time he is adult, he has achieved a certain height and type of body build. Differences in such characteristics, involving the size, shape, and color of the body or of different parts of it are *physical differences*. These differences have been used by anthropologists (scientists who specialize in the study of man) to divide human beings into various races.

SKIN

One way of dividing people into races is to consider the color of the skin. The example we are most familiar with in America is that of the Negro and the white man. In Chapter 1 we pointed out how impossible it is to draw a sharp line between these two groups. Still, most Negroes look sufficiently different from most white men so that you can tell one from the other without difficulty.

Furthermore, skin color is decided from birth. A Negro child may grow up to be a skillful writer, or an excellent lawyer or scientist, perhaps even a member of Congress or a Nobel Prize winner, but the color of his skin doesn't change. He is still a Negro.

Now the color of normal human skin is due to the presence of three kinds of colored chemicals, or *pigments*. The most important of these pigments is *melanin*, a dark-brown substance. *The skin of all normal human beings contains melanin.* Some persons, of course, possess more melanin than others. White men, generally, have little melanin in their skin. Those who have very little have fair complexions. Those with somewhat more are darker. Negroes, naturally, have more melanin in their skins than white men. It is not a question, then, of different colors, but only of greater or smaller amounts of the same color.

The second of the three pigments is *carotene*. This is a yellow substance which is present in carrots (from which it gets its name) and egg yolk as well as in

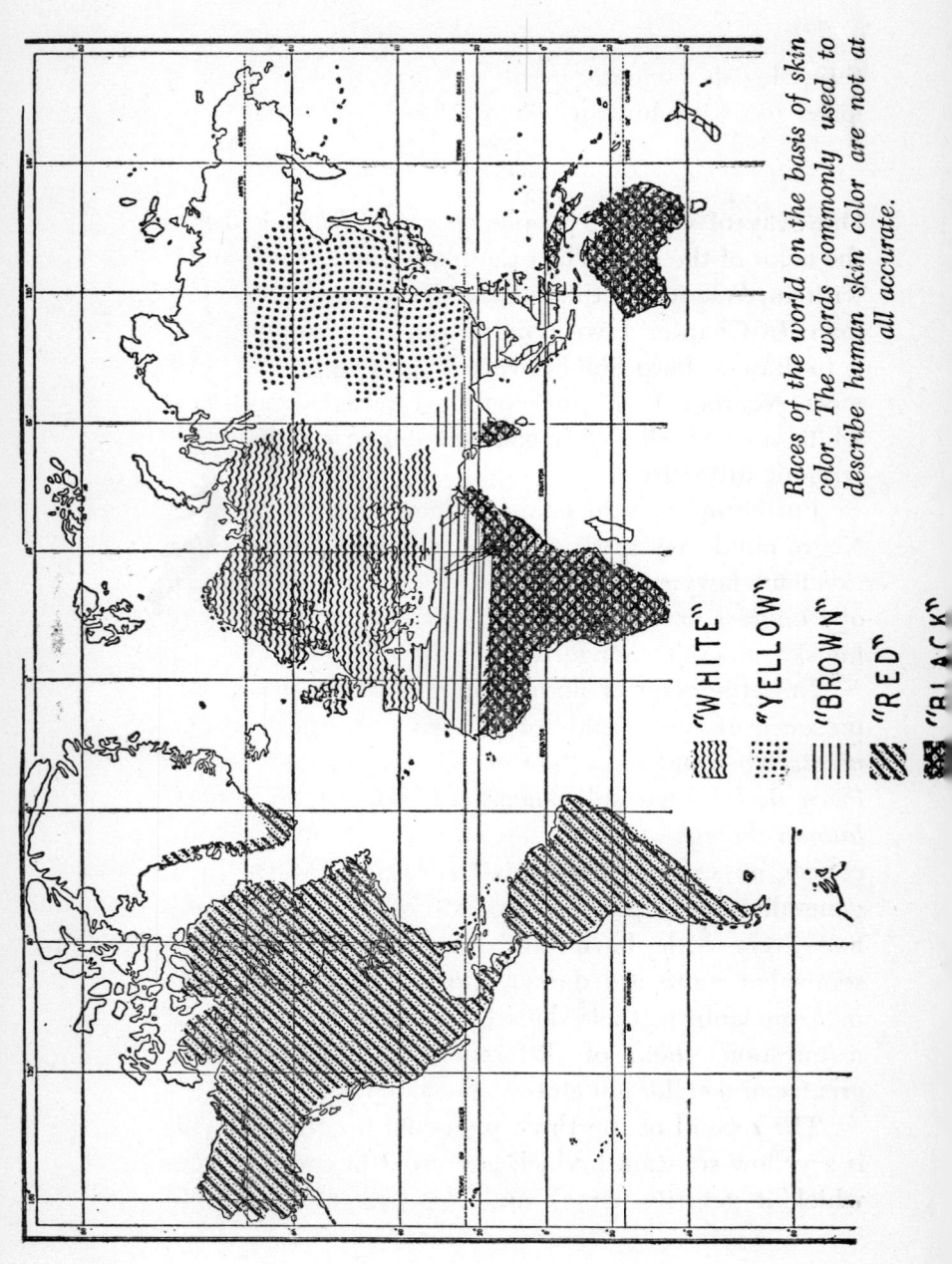

Races of the world on the basis of skin color. The words commonly used to describe human skin color are not at all accurate.

human skin. Like melanin, carotene occurs in the skin of all human beings. Because of its rather light color, its presence is not visible in people with considerable melanin in the skin. The melanin covers it up. Among people with little melanin in the skin, some have more carotene and some have less. Those with more carotene, such as the peoples of eastern Asia, have a somewhat yellowish complexion.

The third pigment is *hemoglobin,* which is the red coloring matter of blood. Naturally, all human beings possess that, too. However, the hemoglobin occurs in the blood vessels beneath the skin, so that very little can show through. The presence of fair amounts of either melanin or carotene in the skin covers it up completely. Hemoglobin does show up, however, in the skin of white men, particularly in those of light complexion. It is the hemoglobin that accounts for pink cheeks and the ability to blush.

On the basis of these differences in coloring, mankind is sometimes divided into (1) a "Black Race," high in melanin; (2) a "Yellow Race," low in melanin but high in carotene; and (3) a "White Race," low in both melanin and carotene.

This would seem a neat and satisfactory division, but there are certain difficulties. For one thing, the differences aren't sharp. There are all sorts of intermediate colors. The inhabitants of Southeast Asia and the original Indian inhabitants of the Americas, for instance, are darker than the Chinese and Japanese members of the "Yellow Race." On the other hand, they do not seem to be Negroes. Sometimes the Southeast Asians as well as the inhabitants of many of the Pacific islands are said to be members of a "Brown Race," while the American Indians are a "Red Race." (This last is a particularly poor description, since Indians aren't red at all but brownish.) In other respects, however, these peoples are known to be rather similar to the "Yellow Race"; so perhaps a better solution would be to speak of a "Yellow-Brown Race" including all these groups.

Another source of confusion is that groups of people may have similar skin colors and yet be different in many other ways. There are the dark-skinned peoples of Africa, called the Negroes, and the dark-skinned original inhabitants of Australia, called the Aborigines. The average Aboriginal is even darker than the average Negro, but to call them both simply members of the "Black Race" is to miss a point. In many physical characteristics other than skin color the African Negro and the Australian Aboriginal are quite different. There is a third dark-skinned group of people, called the Dravidians, who were among the earliest inhabitants of India and who are now concentrated in the southern areas of that country. Despite their dark skins, they are different in many respects from both the Negroes and the Aborigines.

Nor are all native Africans of the "Black Race" as dark-skinned as we imagine. Americans are accustomed to dark-skinned Negroes because the ancestors of most American Negroes were brought to America from West Africa. That happens to be a region of particularly dark-skinned peoples. There are Negroes that are much lighter in color. Some East African tribes, for instance, are light-brown, almost yellowish, in color.

Then, too, skin color is not completely unchanging.

Though skins cannot be made to grow lighter, they can often be darkened quite easily by the natural process of sun-tanning. The ultraviolet rays of the sun can be quite harmful to the skin if it penetrates the outer layers. (Many of us know by first-hand experience how painful sunburn is.) Melanin, by blocking the ultraviolet rays, protects the skin. Many members of the "White Race," without enough melanin in the skin for protection, can develop additional melanin with time if they work or play with skin exposed to the sun. (This development is rather slow, and that is why over-exposure at first will cause sunburn.) Very fair-complexioned people often lack the capacity to develop enough melanin under any circumstances. They burn but do not tan.

The skin of a sun-tanned man will fade slowly once his exposure to the sun stops. Still, many a sun-tanned member of the "White Race" actually has more melanin in his skin than many an African member of the "Black Race."

HAIR

Hair color, unlike skin color, has not been used to divide mankind into races. The most important pigment of hair, as of skin, is melanin. A large majority of human beings possess enough melanin in their hair to make it dark brown or black. Some members of the "White Race" have so little melanin that their hair is light brown or even blond. There is a red pigment in some hair, and its color shows up in light-haired people to give the various shades of red hair. With age, the ability to form melanin for the new hairs that are continually replacing old hairs is often lost. The result is then gray or even white hair.

In Europe and North America, where modern theories of race developed, the various shades of hair are so numerous and scattered that people just don't pay much attention to them. To be sure, the Germanic-speaking peoples who invaded western and southern Europe in the sixth century were of lighter complexion than the Romance-speaking peoples they conquered. Until mixing became virtually complete, there was therefore more blond hair among the aristocratic descendants of the invaders than among the peasant descendants of the conquered. It may be for that reason that the princesses in fairy tales (many of which originated during the Middle Ages) are frequently described as having blond hair.

Leaving color to one side, however, some anthropologists have tried to classify human beings into races according to the form of hair they possess. Hair can be straight, it can be wavy, or it can be kinky.

Virtually all members of the "Yellow-Brown Race," for example, have straight hair, without a trace of wave or kink. The Eskimos, whom most people would consider "Yellow," also have straight hair, but so do the Turkish peoples of central and western Asia, many of whom, particularly in western Asia, seem "White."

Kinky, or woolly, hair—that is, hair which is arranged in very tight curls—is characteristic of members of the "Black Race" who are native to Africa and to New Guinea and neighboring islands.

Wavy hair occurs among members of the "White

Race" and also among the dark Dravidians of India and the very dark Aborigines of Australia.

Here, too, things are not quite as simple as they look at first. Many Europeans (or Americans of European descent) have perfectly straight hair although they belong to the "wavy-haired" group. On the other hand, there are at least three kinds of kinky hair. There is short kinky hair that covers the whole scalp evenly, as with most Negro peoples. There is short kinky hair that grows in tufts with seemingly bare spaces between, as in some East African groups. Then there is the longer kinky hair of the peoples of the Southwest Pacific islands. The hair of the Australian Aborigines is curly or wavy, except for one small group in Queensland who have what is called "frizzy" hair, or hair that is slightly kinky.

EYES

Eye color, like hair color, is not used for distinguishing races. The pigment of the iris (which is the colored portion of the eye), like that of the hair and skin, is melanin. In most human beings there is enough melanin in the eye to make it appear brown. Those who possess very little melanin have blue eyes.

There is one peculiarity of eye structure which has been used in making racial distinctions—the *epicanthic eye-fold*. This is a fold of flesh that covers the upper eyelid, and sometimes even the upper eyelashes, when the eyes are wide open. It gives the eyes a narrow appearance and is sometimes wrongly referred to as "slant eyes."

The epicanthic eye-fold is possessed by many members of the "Yellow-Brown Race," such as the Chinese, Japanese, Mongols, and Eskimos, but not by all. It does not commonly occur in the other groups of people we have mentioned.

BONES

Next to skin color, bone structure is most often used in making distinctions between one human being and another. Bones form the hard framework of the human body, and it is the bony structure that is responsible for the fact that one person is tall and has narrow shoulders while another person is short and has stubby fingers. (Naturally, layers of fat will also affect a person's appearance, but that is easily altered by diet.)

Height is a common way of distinguishing peoples. There are short individuals and tall individuals in all groups of people. Still, the average height among Scandinavians is considerably more than the average height among Sicilians. The people of northern France are, on the average, somewhat taller than the people of southern France.

Members of the "Yellow-Brown" and "Black" races can also be divided into various groups of different heights. The Chinese are taller than the Japanese. The African peoples show great variety. Some Negro tribes are as tall as or taller than the Scandinavians. The Pygmies of the Congo, on the other hand, are the shortest people (as a group) known.

There are numerous difficulties in this matter of height, however. In the first place, the height of an individual can't be known until he is fully grown; so height is useless in classifying children. Furthermore, there are, as we have said, short individuals in all groups, and a particular Sicilian may be taller than a particular Scandinavian. In addition to this, height differs with sex, men usually being considerably taller than the women of the same group. Finally, height varies with such things as diet. The children of European immigrants to America often grow to be taller than their parents, probably because their diet is better.

HEADS

The particular set of bones most often measured for purposes of racial classification are those of the head. As seen from above, the head has an oval shape, which is longer in one direction (from front to back) than in the other (from side to side). If the front-to-back length of the head is called 100, then the side-to-side width is equal to some smaller figure. If the width were three-quarters of the length, it would be 75; if it were four-fifths of the length, it would be 80.

The width of the head in relation to the length is known as the *cephalic index*. Naturally, the cephalic index is different for different people. People with a cephalic index of less than 75 have long, narrow skulls, as seen from above, since the width of the skull is less than three-quarters of its length. People with skulls of this shape are called *dolichocephalic,* which is simply Greek for "long-headed." If the cephalic index is more than 80, the head appears to be short and broad, as seen from above. People with skulls of this shape are called *brachycephalic,* which is the Greek for "short-headed." A cephalic index between 75 and 80 makes a

HEAD SHAPES

A DOLICHOCEPHALIC HEAD

A MESOCEPHALIC HEAD

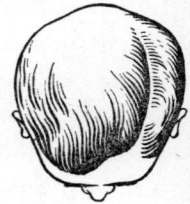
A BRACHYCEPHALIC HEAD

head *mesocephalic,* which is Greek for "medium-headed."

Groups of people can differ from one another in head shape. The peoples in northwestern Europe, including the inhabitants of Scandinavia, Great Britain, Holland, Belgium, and the northern portions of France and Germany, are medium-headed, on the average. The peoples farther south, in central France, southern Germany, and northern Italy (as well as almost all the people of eastern Europe) are short-headed. Still farther south, along the Mediterranean, in Portugal, Spain, southern France, Italy, and the Balkans, the people are medium-headed. In North Africa and the Middle East many long-heads are found.

Using such skull measurements as a guide, some people have attempted to divide the "White Race" into three sub-races. The people of northwestern Europe they call *Nordic.* These are light-complexioned medium-heads. The people of central and eastern Europe are *Alpine.* These are dark-complexioned short-heads. Finally, the people of southern Europe and northern

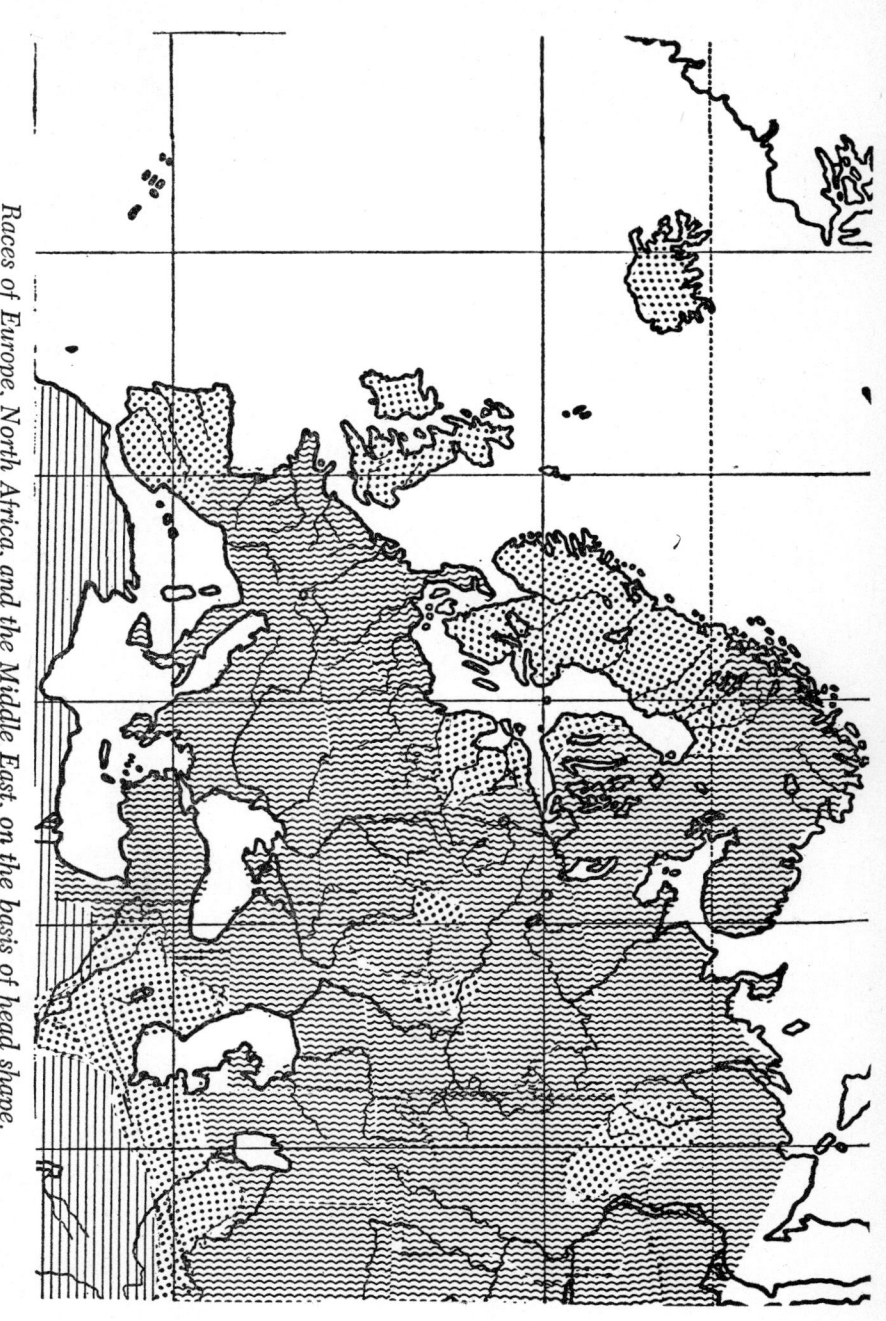

Races of Europe, North Africa, and the Middle East, on the basis of head shape.

Africa are *Mediterranean*. These are dark-complexioned medium-heads and long-heads.

Under such a system, some European countries would be inhabited mostly by one such "sub-race." For instance, Norway would be almost entirely Nordic, Hungary almost entirely Alpine, and Portugal almost entirely Mediterranean. Other countries would be made up of two or even three "sub-races." Germany contains both Nordics and Alpines. Italy contains both Alpines and Mediterraneans. France, which has a population that is quite uniform culturally, would be made up of all three of these "sub-races."

Head shapes vary outside the "White Race" too. Most members of the "Black Race" are long or medium-headed and most members of the "Yellow-Brown Race" are short-headed.

The shape of the head, like height, can vary with the diet. Children born during a long northern winter are deprived of sunlight during the early months of their lives. Unless they are given cod-liver oil or some form of vitamin preparation, they are apt to be lacking in Vitamin D. When this happens, the children suffer from a disease known as *rickets,* in which bones do not harden properly. The too soft skulls of such children may then become misshapen from the pressure of the cradle, and skull measurements in later life won't mean much.

ARE PHYSICAL DIFFERENCES THE ANSWER?

So far, the physical differences we have discussed all seem to have certain faults as clues to racial classification. We can list some of these faults.

1. The characteristics we have discussed—skin color, hair form, height, and skull shape—cannot be divided into neat groups. The extremes fade into one another. There are always people of medium height and people who are "middle-headed." There are people who are only moderately dark-skinned, or who have hair that is only slightly wavy or slightly kinky. For that reason there are always questions as to whether an individual or even a group of individuals belongs to one race or to another.

2. Some of the characteristics vary with such things as diet and exposure to the sun. The form of hair can be altered by chemical treatment. (You have heard of "permanent waves." There are also methods for straightening kinky hair.)

3. The different characteristics divide mankind in different ways. If we go by skin color, the Dravidians are lumped with the Negroes. If we go by hair form, the Dravidians are lumped with the Europeans. If we classify men by height and shape of head, the Nordic peoples fall in the same group as many Negro tribes, while the Mediterranean people will be grouped with other Negro tribes. If we use the head shape only, most central Europeans have to be classified with the Japanese.

Actually, then, no single type of physical difference is sufficient. But suppose we use groups of characteristics. In thinking of an African Negro, for instance, we think not only of the dark skin, but also of the flat, broad nose and prominent nostrils, the kinky hair, and the thick lips. A Hindu may have quite dark skin but will possess none of the other characteristics and is not usually considered a Negro. A European may have thick lips, or quite kinky hair, or a broad snub nose and yet not be considered a Negro because he doesn't have a dark enough skin.

Well, then, are such combinations of physical characteristics the answer?

Before we can answer this question, we must consider new problems. Human differences, in order to be useful in determining race, must be passed along to children. You would ordinarily expect children to be of the same race as their parents. In fact, the chief reason why scientists are interested in the notion of race is the thought that by studying race we can learn how groups of mankind are related. Correct notions of race might tell us something of how man originated and where and how he migrated from place to place before the dawn of written history. Naturally, none of this can be learned unless race is something that can be passed along from parents to children.

Most of the characteristics we have mentioned can be passed along. Chinese children have the epicanthic eye-fold of their parents. Negro children have their parents' dark skin, and so on.

However, this doesn't work out perfectly. Parents with brown eyes will not always have children with brown eyes. Sometimes they have a child with blue eyes. Children of the same parents may be quite different in height or in skull shape. One may be darker in complexion than another, or the hair form may be different. In short, although children usually inherit some of their parents' characteristics, they don't necessarily inherit them all. In fact, they usually don't inherit them all. What's worse, children may have characteristics that don't seem to have come from either the mother's or the father's side of the family.

In order to understand how to use physical differences properly, we will first have to discuss the way the various characteristics are passed on from parents to children. In other words, we will have to talk about the science of *genetics*. In doing so, we will learn how to understand race and racial differences better than we do now. We may even discover certain physical differences which are more useful for defining a race than any of those we have discussed in this chapter.

4

Through the Microscope

DROPS OF LIFE

THE SMALLEST LIVING ANIMALS are tiny creatures called *protozoa* (singular, *protozoön*). Some of these are large enough to be barely visible to the naked eye, but most are too small for the eye. They must therefore be studied under the microscope.

A simple protozoön, such as the *ameba,* consists of a tiny drop of a jelly-like fluid called *protoplasm.* This drop of protoplasm is separated from the water in which the ameba lives by a very thin, very delicate membrane. Protoplasm thus enclosed by a membrane is called a *cell.*

Although the ameba is microscopic in size, it performs all the essential functions of life. It can take in bits of food still smaller than itself, digest them, and discard the indigestible remainder. It can detect danger and can then move about in order to escape from it. It can grow, and when it has grown enough, it can split in two so that two amebas are formed where there was only one before.

When an ameba splits in two, the new "daughter"*

---

* This is a conventional term which does not indicate in any way that the cells are female.

cells have all the characteristics of the old "parent" cell. It is reasonable to think, then, that if we understood how a cell divides into two cells, keeping its characteristics, we might make a start toward learning how characteristics are passed on in larger creatures such as men.

A protozoön is made up of a single cell. Animals larger than protozoa are made up of a number of cells packed close together. Since each of these cells is of about the same size as the cell of a protozoön, it takes a considerable number of them to make up a large animal. The human being, for instance, consists of trillions upon trillions of microscopic cells. Each human cell is made up of protoplasm; each is surrounded by a cell membrane. Animals made up of a number of cells are *metazoa*. Man is a *metazoön*.

The single cell of the protozoön is a jack-of-all-trades kind of cell. It can do a little of everything. In metazoa, the different cells specialize. In the human being, for instance, there are long, thin muscle cells which become short and thick when the muscle contracts. There are nerve cells with jagged outlines which pass messages from one part of the body to another. There are skin cells which serve as a tough protection for the rest of the body.

Some of these different cells such as those which make up the brain and nerves have become so specialized that they have lost the ability to divide. Other kinds of cells, however, continue dividing all through life or, at least, can divide whenever it becomes necessary. For example, the outer cells of the skin gradually wear off in the ordinary course of living. For that reason the cells of the deeper layers of the skin are continually growing and dividing in order to replace the lost cells.

The process by which human cells divide is much the same as that by which protozoa divide. Human cells retain their characteristics after dividing, just as protozoa do. In fact, the process of division is approximately the same in all cells. In order to investigate the process, let's look inside the cell.

To begin with, all cells that grow and divide consist of two parts. Somewhere within the cell, often near its center, is a small spot of protoplasm which is marked off from the rest of the cell by a membrane even thinner and more delicate than the cell's outer membrane. This inner portion of the cell is called the *nucleus*. The protoplasm surrounding it is the *cytoplasm*.

The nucleus is the more important of the two parts of the cell. Suppose an ameba is divided in two by a microscopic needle-point in such a way that one half of it contains the whole nucleus while the other half contains none of the nucleus. The half with the nucleus will grow back the missing part and will live normally thereafter, growing and dividing. The half without the nucleus lives for a short while but then shrivels up and dies. It does not grow and never divides.

Well, then, let's look inside the nucleus. If we make very thin slices of some body tissue and place them under the microscope, we can see individual cells and even, perhaps, the nuclei within the cells. If we confine ourselves to just looking, however, there isn't much to see inside the nucleus. But we needn't confine ourselves to just looking.

The nucleus, like the cell as a whole, is made up of

CELLS

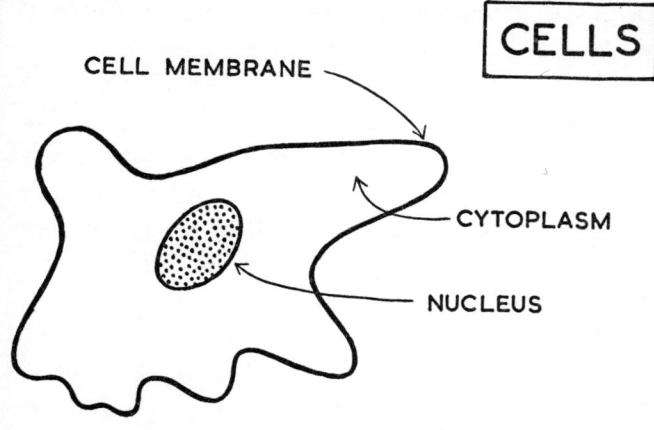

AMEBA (A ONE-CELLED CREATURE)

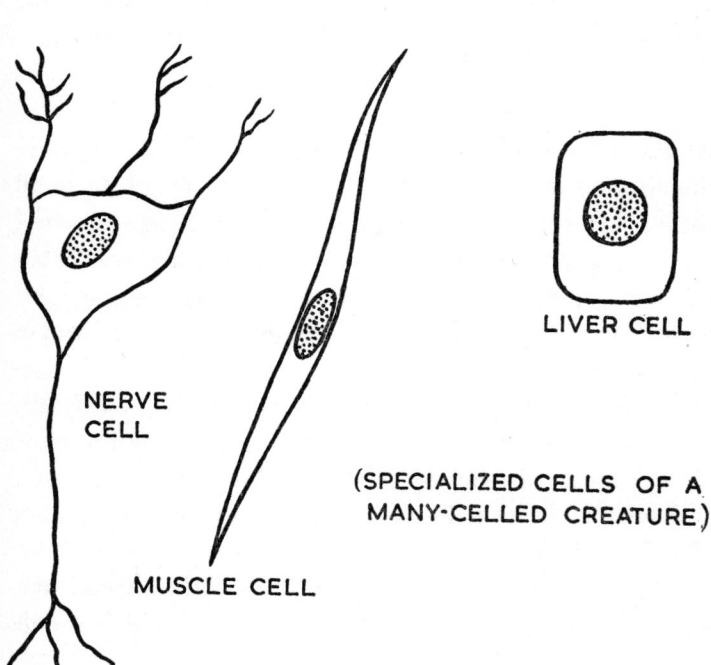

(SPECIALIZED CELLS OF A MANY-CELLED CREATURE)

a vast number of different substances. Certain chemical preparations, when added to the water in which a tissue slice is placed, can leak into the cells within the slice and combine with some, but not all, of the substances it finds there. The chemical combinations which are formed are sometimes colored. By adding the proper chemical preparation to the tissue slice, we succeed in coloring some parts of the cell and not others.

When a preparation known as *Feulgen reagent* is added to the cell, scattered portions of the nucleus turn a deep red. These portions are called *chromatin* (from a Greek word meaning "color"). If the preparation is added to cells at different stages of division, the behavior of the chromatin can be followed, and it is this chromatin behavior which is the key to the situation.

HOW CELLS DIVIDE

At the very beginning of the process of cell division, the chromatin of the nucleus begins collecting into small thread-like forms. These threads of chromatin are called *chromosomes*. The number of chromosomes varies in the cells of different kinds of animals. There is a kind of fly with only eight chromosomes in its cells and a kind of crayfish with over a hundred. In any one kind of animal, all cells (with an exception we'll talk about in the next chapter) have the same number of chromosomes. In human cells, for instance, chromatin collects into exactly 48 chromosomes during the process of cell division.

Because chromatin collects into little thread-like forms during cell division, the process by which a cell

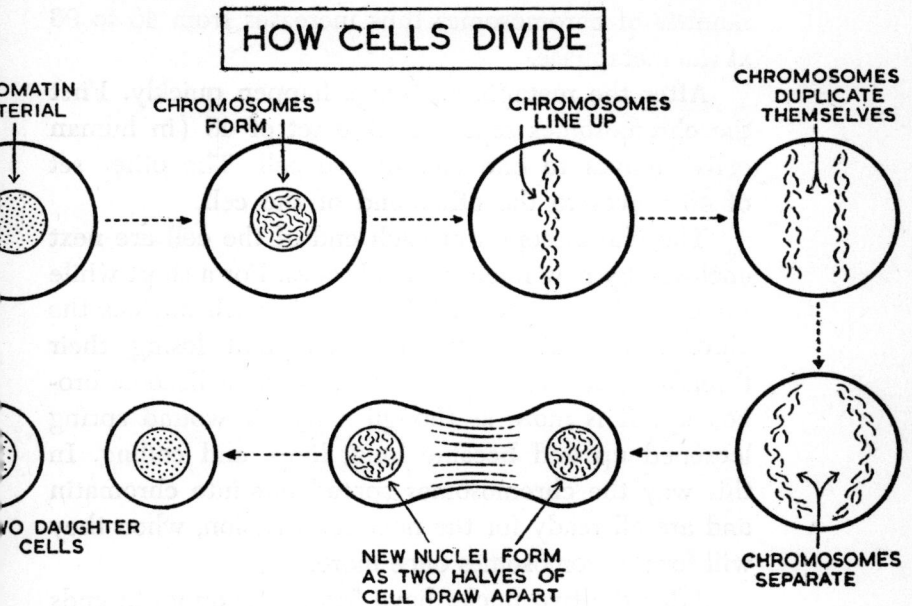

divides is called *mitosis*, from the Greek word for "thread."

After the chromosomes have been formed, the nuclear membrane disappears, and the material of the nucleus mixes with the material of the cytoplasm. The chromosomes, meanwhile, spread out across the middle of the cell.

This is the crucial moment. It is called the *metaphase*. The chromosomes remain in the middle of the cell, and after a while each chromosome is suddenly accompanied by a companion chromosome lined up immediately next to it. In the dividing human cell, the number of chromosomes thus increases from 48 to 96 at the metaphase.

After the metaphase, things happen quickly. First the chromosomes separate. One set of 48 (in human cells) moves to one end of the cell. The other set of 48 moves to the other end of the cell.

The chromosomes at each end of the cell are next enclosed by new nuclear membranes. For a short while the cell possesses two nuclei. Within each nucleus the chromosomes start spreading out and losing their thread-like shape. They do not dissolve or become broken up. It is more as though a tightly wound spring loosened up and became long, limp, and coiling. In this way the chromosomes spread out into chromatin and are all ready for the next cell division, when they will form chromosomes once more.

After the two nuclei have formed at opposite ends of the cell, the cell begins to pinch at the middle. The middle grows narrower and narrower until the cell pinches apart altogether. In protozoa the two resulting cells move away from each other and become two separate individuals. In metazoa the two daughter cells must remain in place. A new cell membrane, however, now separates the two parts of what had once been one cell.

Now let us get back to the metaphase. The one unusual thing about the entire process of mitosis is the doubling of the chromosomes. Everything else is simply a matter of dividing the substance of a cell into two equal portions and separating these from each other by a membrane.

You may ask: "Isn't that what happens to the chromosomes, too? Doesn't each chromosome simply split down its length and become two chromosomes?"

Well, in order to answer that question, it isn't enough to get inside the cell, or even inside the nucleus. We have to get inside the chromosome.

INSIDE THE CHROMOSOME

We are now dealing with objects that are so small that we have to pause to consider how much smaller we can get, anyway. As we probably all know in these days of the A-bomb, all matter is composed of *atoms*. Atoms are exceedingly small objects. A chromosome which is just big enough to be seen with a microscope is still big enough to contain many billions of atoms.

Atoms are of a hundred different types, some being more common than others. With rare exceptions, atoms are bound together in groups. Sometimes a group consists of only one kind of atom. More often a group consists of two or more different kinds of atoms. Sometimes the groups may be made up of only two atoms each, sometimes of half a dozen, sometimes of several million. In any case, a group of atoms, whether it consists of one kind or of many, whether it contains two atoms or two million, is called a *molecule*.

Every different type of substance known (and there are many hundreds of thousands of such) is made up of its own kind of molecule. Every different kind of molecule has its own set of properties and characteristics.

For instance, if you divide a lump of matter, such as sugar, in two, each part will still be sugar. If you keep on dividing the sugar into smaller and smaller pieces, each fragment is still sugar. Even if it were possible to divide the sugar so finely as to separate it into single molecules (billions of trillions of them), each molecule would be sugar. The molecule, however, is the smallest particle which can retain the characteristics of the substance it makes up. If you were to divide a molecule of sugar in two, you would be left with two collections of atoms, each half as large as the original molecule. Neither of the new collections would be sugar, however.

It's as though you took a class of 16 pupils and divided it in two. You would then have two classes of 8 pupils each. You could continue the process and make 4 classes of 4 pupils each, 8 classes of 2 pupils each, or even 16 classes of 1 pupil each. You would have to stop there, though. If you were to try to carry the process one step further and form 32 classes of half a pupil each, you would end up with no classes at all, no pupils, and considerable trouble with the police.

Now let us get back to the chromosome. A chromosome is made up of a substance called *nucleoprotein*. The nucleoprotein molecule is of tremendous size compared with most molecules. It is a million or more times as large as the sugar molecule. (Even so it is still too small to be seen under ordinary microscopes.) The chromosome is a string of several thousand of these giant nucleoprotein molecules arranged in single file.

Now imagine what would happen if each chromosome were to split down the middle at the metaphase and become two chromosomes. It would be like splitting a string of pearls down the middle. You wouldn't

INSIDE THE CHROMOSOME

have two strings of pearls, merely two sets of half-pearls, worth nothing. Or it would be like splitting a column of boys down the long way, which is also not a good idea.

We can now answer the question which ended the previous section. Chromosomes do *not* simply split down the middle, becoming two chromosomes at the metaphase. If a chromosome were split down the middle each nucleoprotein molecule would be destroyed. Instead of having two chromosomes, you would have none.

In order, then, for every chromosome to become two chromosomes at the metaphase, one chromosome has to be created out of simpler materials.

How is this done? Well, nobody knows exactly. Many scientists are studying the process. Once they learn the complete answer, they will have in their possession one of the important keys to the knowledge of the nature of life itself.

Roughly, though, what seems to happen is this: The protoplasm within a cell contains various simple substances which can be put together to form a chromosome. (Like jigsaw pieces, you see, which, when properly put together, can form a large picture.) Some of these substances are called *amino acids*. Others are called *purines, pyrimidines, pentoses,* and *phosphate ions*. In some way these simple substances are drawn out of the protoplasm and lined up near the various chromosomes. The line-up is such that every amino acid in each chromosome has a similar amino acid in position next to it; every purine has a similar purine for a neighbor, and so on. When the line-up is completed,

HOW NEW CHROMOSOMES ARE FORMED

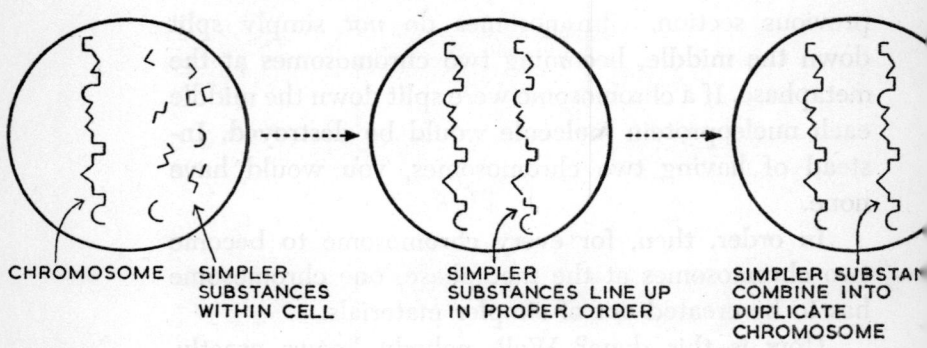

CHROMOSOME | SIMPLER SUBSTANCES WITHIN CELL | SIMPLER SUBSTANCES LINE UP IN PROPER ORDER | SIMPLER SUBSTANCES COMBINE INTO DUPLICATE CHROMOSOME

all these small molecules and ions are joined together, and then we have a second chromosome next to the first. Since the second chromosome is made up of exactly the same molecules and ions as the first, lined up in exactly the same order, it is a duplicate of the first chromosome. The first chromosome has acted as a kind of model on which a second is fashioned.

The process by which a chemical structure forms another structure just like itself out of the materials in the protoplasm is known as *autoreproduction*.

To summarize, then, what happens at the metaphase in a dividing human cell is that each of the forty-eight chromosomes in the cell autoreproduces. A second set of chromosomes is formed which is an exact duplicate of the first set. The two sets move to opposite ends of the cell, and when the cell divides each daughter cell has its own set of chromosomes.

ENZYMES AND GENES

We have seen that a cell contains a variety of different substances that can be used as raw materials in the manufacture of complicated structures such as chromosomes. Every cell, in fact, contains within its microscopic structure many thousands of different chemicals. These chemicals are continually colliding and combining with one another, exchanging atoms, splitting apart, rearranging the atoms within their own structure, and so on. Activities such as these are referred to as *chemical reactions*.

It may seem to you from this description that events within a cell must be very confusing, a mishmash, like people running every which way in a busy railroad station. However, there is one type of molecule which brings order and sense into the chemical reactions taking place within the cell. These are the *enzymes*. Enzymes are large molecules which are capable of influencing the way in which certain chemical reactions take place. Each enzyme can influence one particular chemical reaction; so in its vicinity only that one proceeds and no other.

Within the cell, various enzymes seem to be located in orderly fashion. For instance, many enzymes are part of small structures within the cytoplasm of a cell. These structures are called *mitochondria*. Like the chromosomes, the mitochondria are composed of a nucleoprotein. The nucleoprotein of mitochondria is, however, of a different type, chemically, from that of the chromosomes.

We can look upon a cell as something like a microscopic factory. Molecules of all sorts enter the body from the air and from the food we eat and are carried to the individual cells by the blood stream. This is similar to the way in which coal, steel, rubber, and other raw materials are carried to factories by trains and ships.

Inside the cell, these molecules are broken down to release energy or are built up to form more complicated molecules. This is similar to the way in which factories burn coal to obtain energy or use steel and other materials to build up a complicated structure like an automobile or an airplane. Every chemical reaction in the cell is controlled by an enzyme, just as every operation in a factory is controlled by some workman. The enzymes are organized along mitochondria, just as workers are organized along assembly lines.

Just as a factory could accomplish nothing by itself if all the workers were out on strike, so a cell could accomplish nothing without its thousands of enzymes. Well, then, where do the enzymes come from? That is an important question. The best answer that we know so far is this: *Enzymes are formed by the nucleoprotein molecules within the chromosomes.*

As we have said, a chromosome does not consist of a single nucleoprotein molecule, but of thousands of such molecules strung out in a line. Each separate nucleoprotein molecule is called a *gene*.

Genes have two important properties. One is the ability to autoreproduce during mitosis, the process explained in the sections, *How Cells Divide* and *Inside the Chromosome*. The other is the ability to produce an enzyme. Exactly how it does this is not yet known. Perhaps all of a gene is used as a model for another gene, and only a certain part of a gene is used as a model for an enzyme.

Some scientists believe that every gene has the capacity to form one particular enzyme and no other. Others are not completely convinced that genes are quite so specialized. It seems fairly certain, however, that the exact nature of the genes present in the chromosomes of a cell will determine the nature of the enzymes present in the cell. Since the enzymes supervise chemical reactions, the genes control the chemistry of the cell. After cell division, each daughter cell has identical genes and therefore identical chemistries. That is the result of autoreproduction in mitosis: both daughter cells have identical genes.

GENES AND PHYSICAL CHARACTERISTICS

Now that we have shown how cells retain their characteristics after dividing, you may wonder how this applies to the problem of human races. The application is just this: the physical characteristics we mentioned in the previous chapter are determined by cell chemistry. Anything that affects cell chemistry can affect, one way or another, the physical characteristics of the body.

As an example, let us consider skin color.

The large molecule of the pigment melanin is formed in the skin cells from a much smaller molecule called *tyrosine*. (Tyrosine is colorless and is present in all cells.) The steps of the process are not all known, but one of the early steps that are known requires the presence of an enzyme called *tyrosinase*. In the skin cells of most human beings there is at least one gene whose job it is to manufacture tyrosinase. If the gene is of a type that can form considerable quantities of tyrosinase, the skin cell is like a well-staffed factory. Considerable quantities of melanin are formed, and the person possessing that gene therefore has a dark-brown skin, black hair, and dark-brown eyes. If the gene were of a type that manufactured only a small amount of tyrosinase, the reverse would be true. Little melanin would be formed, and the person would have fair skin, light hair, and light eyes.

There are some people, moreover, whose genes do not form tyrosinase at all. No tyrosinase occurs in their cells, and therefore no melanin can be formed. Such people have very fair skin, white hair, and no pigment at all in their eyes. (Their eyes look reddish because small blood vessels can be seen through the transparent colorless iris of the eye.) Such people are called *albinos*. If you have ever met an albino, you have seen for yourself what a startling effect on physical appearance the absence of only one gene can have.

Actually there are other enzymes, and therefore other genes, involved in the formation of melanin. Skin color is for that reason more complicated than it would seem from what we have said so far.

Another physical characteristic we might consider is height. One of the factors that influence a person's height is a chemical known as the *growth hormone*. This substance is formed in the cells of a small structure called the *pituitary gland*, which is located just underneath the brain. The growth hormone seeps from the pituitary gland into the blood stream. The blood carries it to all parts of the body, and somehow (again we don't know the exact details) the chemical encourages cells to grow and divide.

If there are no other factors to be considered (such as diet or disease), a person with more growth hormone in his blood will grow more quickly than one with less growth hormone. He will probably end by growing larger and taller. There are some people in whom, for some reason, very little growth hormone is produced by the pituitary gland. Such a person scarcely grows at all, and the result is what is known as a *midget*. Contrariwise, some people have a particularly large supply of growth hormone, and they grow into *giants*. The midgets and giants we see in circus sideshows are the result of a lack and a surplus of the growth hormone.

The growth hormone is formed in the pituitary gland under the supervision of enzymes. The amount of growth hormone formed therefore depends, in part at least, on the amount of certain enzymes formed in the cells. That, in turn, depends on the nature of the genes in charge of forming those enzymes. And so the height, like the skin color, goes back to the nature of the genes a person possesses.

Similar arguments can be advanced for any physical characteristic. It is always a question of the gene. For that reason it is logical to suppose that, if we are to succeed in dividing people into racial groups, we must first learn all we can about how genes are passed from parents to children.

5

From Parent to Child

THE EGG CELL AND THE SPERM CELL

ALL NORMAL ANIMALS, except the very simplest, produce special cells which have the ability to develop into new individuals under the proper circumstances. Such cells produced by female animals are known as *egg cells*. The egg cell is often called by the Latin word for "egg," which is *ovum* (plural, *ova*).

The egg cell with which we are most familiar is that produced by the hen. You can see at once one way in which an egg cell differs from other cells. Consider the size of a hen's egg, and remember that it is all a single cell. Compare this with cells which are so small that a microscope is required to see them. To be sure, only a microscopic spot on the surface of the yolk of the egg is really alive. All the rest is simply a food supply. It takes the chick three weeks to grow from that microscopic spot to a little creature completely filling the shell. The egg must contain all the calories, vitamins, and minerals the chick will need for those three weeks.

In human beings (and in other mammals, too) the situation is somewhat different. The egg cell develops within the body of the mother. Very soon after the egg cell starts developing, a structure known as the *placenta* is formed. In the placenta, the blood vessels of the developing child approach very closely to the blood vessels of the mother. Food, air, vitamins, and all the necessities of life leak across from the mother's blood to the child's blood. In this way the mother nourishes the child. (Please take special note of the fact that the blood vessels of mother and child approach but do not join! There is no mingling of blood!)

Since the human mother's blood stream nourishes the developing child, there is no need for the human ovum to contain much food. It is therefore much

MALE AND FEMALE SEX CELLS

NUCLEUS

HEAD

TAIL

HUMAN SPERM CELL

(MALE)

HUMAN EGG CELL

(FEMALE)

smaller than a hen's egg. In fact, the human ovum is only 1/175 of an inch in diameter. Even so, it is still the largest cell in the human body.

Male animals also produce special cells which contribute toward the development of new individuals. These are called *sperm cells* or *spermatozoa* (singular, *spermatozoön*). They are much smaller than egg cells. It would take 600 or more sperm cells to weigh as much as a single egg cell.

The human sperm cell is a very unusual kind of cell, for it can move independently. It does so by means of a long tail, which whips about frantically when the sperm cell is in motion. The tail is about ten times as long as the main portion of the cell. In fact, when a sperm cell is viewed under the microscope, it looks a great deal like a tiny tadpole.

Egg and sperm cells are both produced in special organs. The egg cells are formed in the *ovaries*. All normal females possess two ovaries. Between them, they produce one egg cell about every four weeks. Sperm cells are produced in the *testes*, and all normal males possess two testes. The testes produce vast numbers of sperm cells continuously. A drop of the fluid produced by the testes (the fluid is called *semen*) contains many millions of sperm cells.

When a quantity of semen is liberated near an egg cell, the many sperm cells swim toward it helter-skelter. One sperm cell, and one only, succeeds in entering the egg cell, after penetrating the layer of small cells that surround it. Once a sperm cell has entered the egg cell, no other sperm cell can do so. The combination of egg cell and sperm cell is called a *fertilized ovum*.

There is a world of difference between an egg cell as formed in the ovaries and a fertilized ovum. If an egg cell is not fertilized after having been formed, if no sperm cell comes its way, it is soon broken up and destroyed. It has reached a dead end. A fertilized ovum, however, at once begins to divide and divide again, to grow and develop into an *embryo*. Finally, if all goes well, it is born into the world as a human infant.

Now we can ask ourselves a number of questions. Why are two cells required to produce a new individual? Why must the father and the mother each produce one? Does it matter that the sperm cell is so different in appearance from the egg cell?

In order to answer these questions and others like them, let's turn our attention back to the chromosomes.

TWO HALF-CELLS MAKE A WHOLE CELL

Earlier we said that human cells contain 48 chromosomes. These 48 are arranged in pairs. Every human cell therefore contains 24 pairs of chromosomes. The genes in any chromosome are similar to those in the chromosome paired with it. If one chromosome contains a tyrosinase-forming gene, so does its twin. That gene even occurs in the same place along each chromosome. The genes may not be identical; that is, one may be capable of forming more tyrosinase than the other. Still, both are concerned with the same enzyme.

In other words, the human cell contains 24 different chromosomes, plus a "spare" for each of the 24, making 48 in all.

You may remember that in the previous chapter we said there was one exception to the rule that all human cells contain 48 chromosomes. That exception is the egg cell in the female and the sperm cell in the male.

Egg cells and sperm cells are formed from parent cells containing the usual 48 chromosomes. The parent cells, however, undergo an unusual form of cell division known as *maturation*. The chromosomes do *not* autoreproduce. Instead, the 48 chromosomes simply divide into two groups and travel to opposite ends of the cells. At one end are the 24 different chromosomes and at the other are the 24 "spares."

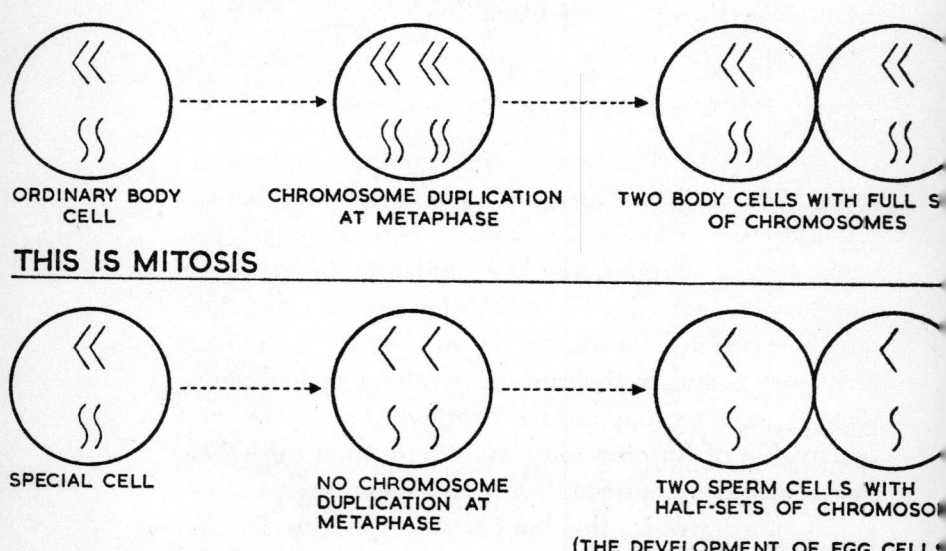

The result is that egg cells and sperm cells are only "half-cells" as far as chromosomes are concerned. They have only 24 chromosomes apiece.

The small sperm cell contains just as many chromosomes, 24, as the much larger egg cell. The sperm cell, however, contains nothing else. It is just 24 chromosomes tightly packed together and driven hither and thither by its lashing tail. The egg cell, on the other hand, contains a considerable quantity of food in addition, on which the embryo can live until the placenta is formed.

When a sperm cell enters an egg cell (leaving its tail outside), it becomes a nucleus, much like the small nucleus in the egg cell. The two nuclei approach and melt into each other. Now the fertilized ovum is a whole cell. It contains 48 chromosomes. That is why a fertilized ovum can develop into an embryo while an unfertilized egg cell cannot. The full number of 48 chromosomes is required.

There is one important difference between the fertilized ovum and all the other cells in the female body in which it exists. The chromosomes are different! Only 24 of the chromosomes of the fertilized ovum were derived from the cells of the female—that is, from the mother. The other 24 chromosomes entered it by way of the sperm cell—that is, from the father.

Now, as the fertilized ovum divides and divides again, every new cell, by the process of autoreproduction, has chromosomes which are identical with those of the original fertilized ovum. The cells of every human being on earth therefore contain 24 chromosomes which are derived from his or her mother and 24 which are

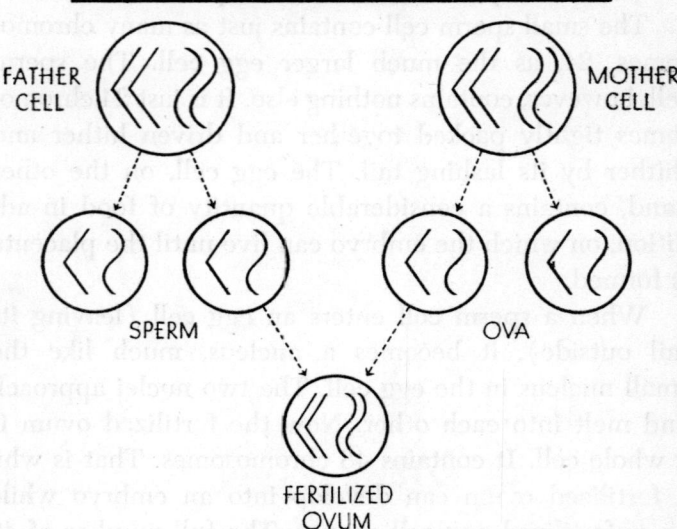

HOW CHROMOSOMES SPLIT UP AND RE-UNITE

FATHER CELL

MOTHER CELL

SPERM

OVA

FERTILIZED OVUM

derived from his or her father. Furthermore, in every pair of chromosomes, one is derived from the mother and one from the father. We can go even further. Every human being has two genes in charge of each particular enzyme, and in each case one is derived from the mother and one from the father. (There are some exceptions to this, as we shall see.)

It doesn't matter that the mother seems to have contributed much more than the father to a child's development. She has contributed an egg cell, which is much heavier than the father's sperm cell. Then, for nine months, it is the mother's blood stream alone that nourishes the growing embryo. Nevertheless, as far as the chromosomes are concerned, each parent makes an equal contribution. And it is the chromosomes that count when it comes to inheriting physical characteristics.

MALE AND FEMALE

The first question anyone asks about a newborn baby is: "Is it a boy or a girl?" You may wonder how long before birth the sex of a baby is determined. The answer to that may surprise you. The sex of the baby is determined at the instant that a sperm cell fertilizes an egg cell.*

Let us see why that is. We have said that all human cells (except egg cells and sperm cells) contain 24 pairs of chromosomes. Actually, that is not entirely correct. The cells of the female do indeed contain 24 perfect pairs. The cells of the male, however, contain 23 perfect pairs, plus a twenty-fourth pair which is a little out of the ordinary. The twenty-fourth pair in males consists of one perfectly good chromosome and one stunted little partner. The full-size chromosome is called the *X-chromosome*. The stunted partner is called the *Y-chromosome*. In other words, the twenty-fourth pair in males does not have a good "spare."

What does this mean in maturation? When an egg cell is formed, the twenty-four pairs of chromosomes in the female divide up evenly. Every egg cell gets twenty-four perfect chromosomes. All egg cells are therefore alike in this respect, and each contains an X-chromosome.

---

* This does not mean the doctor can tell the sex of a baby before it is born. Its sex is determined all right but it is only after birth that we can actually look and see.

When a sperm cell is formed, however, the twenty-four pairs of chromosomes in the male divide up so that one sperm cell gets twenty-four perfect chromosomes and one gets twenty-three perfect chromosomes plus a Y-chromosome. There are, therefore, two kinds of sperm cells, one kind with a Y-chromosome and one kind without. Both kinds are formed in equal numbers.

Now, if an egg cell is fertilized by a sperm without a Y-chromosome, the fertilized ovum ends with twenty-four perfect pairs of chromosomes, and the embryo is automatically female. If an egg cell is fertilized by a sperm with a Y-chromosome, the fertilized ovum ends with twenty-three perfect pairs of chromosomes and a twenty-fourth pair including the Y-chromosome. The embryo is then automatically male.*

Since there are equal numbers of both kinds of sperm cells, there is an equal chance that either kind will fertilize the egg cell, and it is for that reason that there are about as many men in the world as there are women.

Actually, the chances aren't quite 50-50. Male fertilized ova are formed just a little oftener than female fertilized ova are. The reason for this is not yet known.

But there is another factor to be considered. It is useful to have a spare for each chromosome. If something is wrong with a gene on a particular chromo-

* As the fertilized egg divides and re-divides, each new cell is formed in the original pattern. The body cells of a man each have 48 chromosomes, including an X- and a Y-chromosome. The body cells of a woman each have 48 chromosomes, including two X-chromosomes and no Y-chromosome.

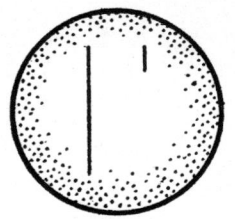
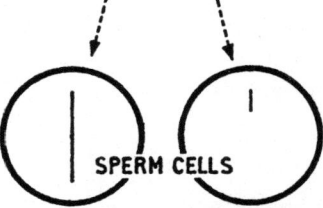
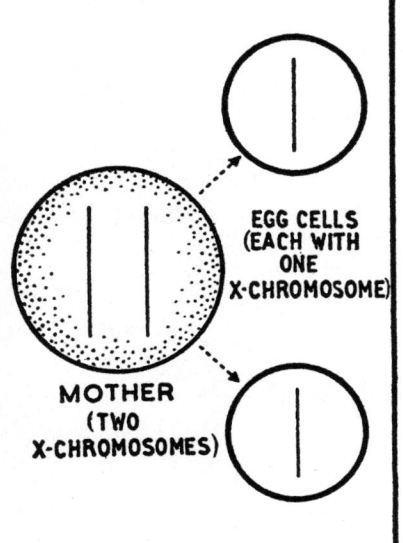
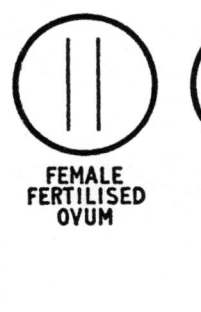
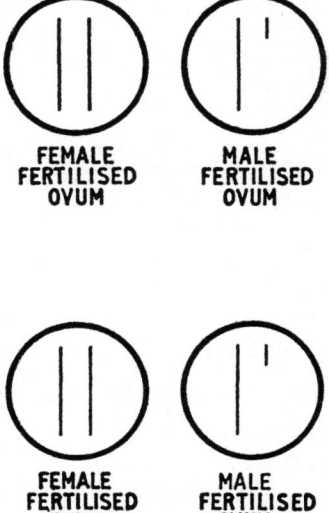

some, the gene on the spare may be perfectly all right, and then the body can usually get along. As far as 23 pairs of chromosomes are concerned, the sexes are equal. In the twenty-fourth chromosome, however, women have an advantage. They have a spare, and men do not. If women have an imperfect gene on the X-chromosome, the spare saves them. If men have an imperfect gene on the X-chromosome, they are out of luck.

It is for this reason, perhaps, that male embryos have a harder time of it than female embryos do. Fewer of them survive to birth. In addition, more male babies die in early infancy than do female babies, and men in general do not live as long as women do. So, despite the fact that more males get started than females, the population has a somewhat higher proportion of women.

In short, men may be taller, heavier, and more muscular than women, but with respect to their chromosomes they are actually the weaker sex.

VARIATIONS AMONG THE GENES

As we have said, genes control enzymes and in that way control the nature of physical characteristics. Unfortunately, we have still very much to learn about the chemistry of the cell. We can hardly ever be certain exactly which enzyme or enzymes control the common physical characteristics. We do know that the enzyme tyrosinase is necessary for the formation of melanin, and therefore determines the color of the skin, hair, and eyes. We are fairly certain, however, that other enzymes are necessary also.

For that reason it is customary to skip the part about the enzyme and just connect the gene with the physical characteristic. For instance, we might talk about the gene for baldness, the gene for five fingers, or the gene for eye color. Sometimes we might wish to speak of various genes which affect the same physical characteristic but in different ways. Eye color is a good example. We could speak of a gene for brown eyes and of one for blue eyes.

A given point on a chromosome can be occupied by only one gene at a time. However, there may be more than one gene capable of occupying that point. When various genes are capable of occupying a certain point on a chromosome, they are said to form a *gene series*. Usually, the different genes of a gene series affect the same physical characteristic, but in different ways. For instance, a tyrosinase-forming gene which is capable of forming considerable tyrosinase will produce brown eyes. A similar gene may occur at that spot in some individuals which is capable of forming only small quantities of tyrosinase and which will produce blue eyes. The gene for brown eyes and the gene for blue eyes are thus two members of a gene series.

Except those on the X- and Y-chromosomes in males, all genes exist in pairs because all chromosomes exist in pairs. For every gene existing on a certain chromosome there is a second gene, governing the same physical characteristic, in the same position on the other chromosome of the pair. The two genes may or may not be identical, however; that is, though they both affect the same physical characteristic, they may affect it in the same way or they may affect it in different ways.

In each cell there are two genes that affect eye color by means of tyrosinase-formation. One is on a certain chromosome, and the other is on the same point on the twin of that chromosome. One may be the brown-eye gene, and so may the other; or one may be the blue-eye gene, and so may the other. Whenever the two genes are identical, the person is said to be *homozygous* for that characteristic. He is homozygous for brown eyes in the first case; he is homozygous for blue eyes in the second case.

But the two genes needn't be identical. They may be different members of the particular gene series. A person may possess the brown-eye gene on one chromosome and the blue-eye gene on its twin. Such a person is *heterozygous* in eye color.

Now "homozygous" and "heterozygous" are hard words. Sometimes people speak of "pure lines" when the two genes are alike and of "hybrids" when they are not alike. These are much simpler terms and familiar ones, too. You may wonder why we don't use them instead. Unfortunately, too many people have the notion that there is something good about being "pure" and something bad about being "hybrid." In order to avoid having trouble with this superstitious notion (actually, as we shall see, there are good and bad points to both conditions), we shall stick to the words "homozygous" and "heterozygous" in this book.

Let us continue to concern ourselves with the eye-color genes. Consider the egg cells that are formed by a woman who is homozygous for brown eyes. The

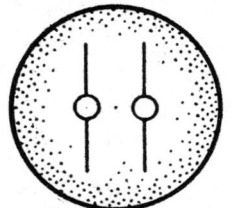

HOW A RECESSIVE GENE SEEMS TO DISAPPEAR

BLUE-EYED PARENT WITH TWO GENES FOR BLUE EYES (HOMOZYGOUS)

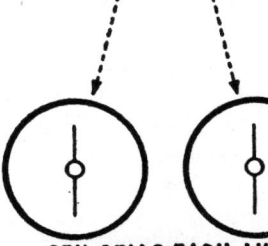

SEX CELLS, EACH WITH ONE GENE FOR BLUE EYES

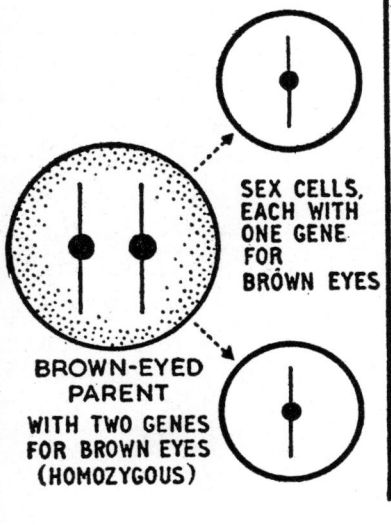

SEX CELLS, EACH WITH ONE GENE FOR BROWN EYES

BROWN-EYED PARENT WITH TWO GENES FOR BROWN EYES (HOMOZYGOUS)

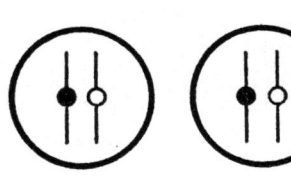

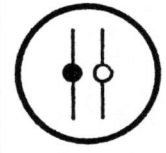

ALL CHILDREN HAVE BROWN EYES AND ARE HETEROZYGOUS, POSSESSING ONE GENE FOR BROWN EYES AND ONE FOR BLUE EYES

chromosome pairs divide, and since the woman has only the brown-eye gene, each egg cell will have one gene for brown eyes. As far as eye color is concerned, all the egg cells will be the same in gene content.

A man who is homozygous for brown eyes will, in the same way, produce sperm cells which have one gene for brown eyes.

Suppose this homozygous man and this homozygous woman are married and have a child. The child will have an eye color that depends upon the nature of the genes in the sperm cell and egg cell which combined to form the fertilized ovum. But, as we explained, all the egg cells contained one gene for brown eyes and all the sperm cells contained one gene for brown eyes. Therefore, no matter which sperm cell fertilizes which egg cell, the fertilized ovum will always have two genes for brown eyes. Like both its parents, the child will be homozygous for brown eyes. So will all other children of this marriage.

If mother and father are both homozygous for blue eyes, then, by the same reasoning, all their children will be homozygous for blue eyes.

But, and this is a great big but, what happens if one parent is homozygous for brown eyes and the other homozygous for blue eyes? Let us say it is the mother who is homozygous for brown eyes. Then every egg cell she produces will contain one gene for brown eyes. The father is homozygous for blue eyes; so each sperm cell he produces will contain one gene for blue eyes. No matter which sperm fertilizes which egg, the fertilized ovum will contain one gene for blue eyes and one gene for brown eyes. The child will be heterozygous.

If it were the father with brown eyes and the mother with blue eyes, the result would be the same. Each egg cell would have one gene for blue eyes, and each sperm cell one gene for brown eyes. Again the fertilized ovum would have one of each, and the child would be heterozygous.

What happens to a child who is heterozygous in eye color? The answer is that he (or she) has brown eyes. You see, the child has one gene which can form large quantities of tyrosinase and one which can form only small quantities. However, the one gene which can form large quantities can form enough, all by itself, to color the eye brown.

The result is that when two parents, one of whom is homozygous for brown eyes and the other homozygous for blue eyes, have children, all the children are heterozygotes having brown eyes. The gene for blue eyes doesn't show. It is invisible. It seems to have disappeared.

When a person possesses two different genes for some physical characteristic at corresponding points of a pair of chromosomes and only one gene seems to show, that gene is called *dominant*. The gene which doesn't show is *recessive*. In the case of eye color, the gene for brown eyes is dominant over the gene for blue eyes. The gene for blue eyes is recessive toward the gene for brown eyes.

It is impossible to tell, just by looking at a person, whether he is homozygous for brown eyes, or whether he is heterozygous in eye color. In either case his eyes are brown. One way of telling the difference is to know something about his parents. If either his mother or his father had blue eyes, he must be heterozygous. Another way of telling is to observe the eye color of his children.

We know already that a person homozygous for brown eyes, if he marries a person homozygous for brown eyes, will have children homozygous for brown eyes. But what if he marries a heterozygous person? The homozygous person (let us suppose it is a man) would form only sperm cells with genes for brown eyes. His heterozygous wife would form egg cells of two types. During maturation, since her cells possess both the brown-eye gene and the blue-eye gene, the brown-eye gene will travel to one end of the cell and the blue-eye gene to the other. Half of the egg cells formed will contain a gene for brown eyes, and half will contain a gene for blue eyes.

The chances are now 50-50 whether a sperm cell will fertilize an egg cell with the brown-eye gene or one with the blue-eye gene. Half of the fertilized ova will be homozygous for brown eyes, and half will be heterozygous. But all of the children will have brown eyes.

Now suppose that both father and mother are heterozygotes. Both would have brown eyes, but both would possess the blue-eye gene. The father would form two kinds of sperm cells, one with the gene for blue eyes and one with the gene for brown eyes. In the same way the mother would form two kinds of egg cells.

Now several combinations of sperm cells and egg

cells are possible. Suppose one of the brown-eye sperm cells fertilizes one of the brown-eye egg cells. The resultant child is homozygous for brown eyes and has brown eyes, naturally. Suppose that a brown-eye sperm cell fertilizes a blue-eye egg cell or that a blue-eye sperm cell fertilizes a brown-eye egg cell. In either case the child is heterozygous and still has brown eyes.

But there is one case left. What if a blue-eye sperm cell fertilizes a blue-eye egg cell? In that case the child is homozygous for blue eyes and has blue eyes!

Thus two brown-eyed parents can have a blue-eyed child. The gene that seemed to have disappeared has appeared once more. Furthermore, you can tell something about the parents. Although their eyes are just as brown as those of a homozygous person, you know they must both be heterozygous or the blue-eye gene couldn't have shown up.

When two persons are similar in some particular physical characteristic, they are said to belong to the same *phenotype*. All people with brown eyes are of the same phenotype as far as eye color is concerned. So are all people with blue eyes. When two persons have the same combination of genes for some particular physical characteristic, they belong to the same *genotype*. Since all blue-eyed people are homozygous, having two genes for blue eyes in their cells, they all have the same combination of genes, and all belong to the same eye-color genotype. Brown-eyed people, however, can be either homozygous or heterozygous. For that reason they belong to two different eye-color genotypes. One genotype includes those with two genes

HOW A RECESSIVE GENE REAPPEARS

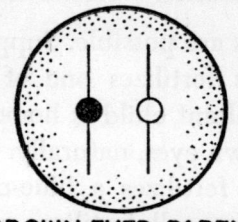

BROWN-EYED PARENT
(HETEROZYGOUS)

SEX CELLS, HALF WITH A GENE FOR BROWN EYES AND HALF WITH A GENE FOR BLUE EYES

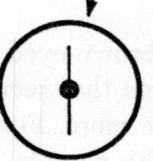 

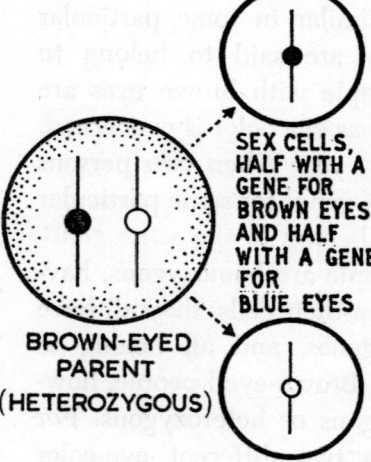

BROWN-EYED PARENT
(HETEROZYGOUS)

SEX CELLS, HALF WITH A GENE FOR BROWN EYES AND HALF WITH A GENE FOR BLUE EYES

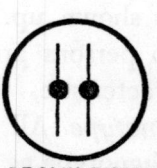

BROWN-EYED CHILD (HOMOZYGOUS)

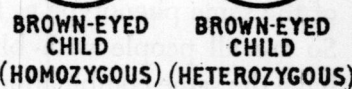

BROWN-EYED CHILD (HETEROZYGOUS)

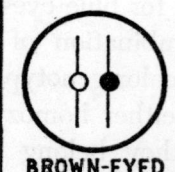

BROWN-EYED CHILD (HETEROZYGOUS)

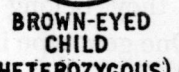

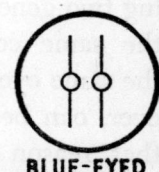

BLUE-EYED CHILD (HOMOZYGOUS)

for brown eyes; the other includes those with one gene for brown eyes and one gene for blue eyes.

You can tell a person's phenotype by looking at him, but you can tell a person's genotype only by examining his parents or his children or both. Sometimes, as we shall see, you can't tell a person's genotype even then.

6

The Rules of Inheritance

MENDEL AND HIS PEAS

UNFORTUNATELY, the inheritance of eye color is not really quite as simple as described in the previous chapter. If it were, people might have noticed the manner in which eye color is inherited much sooner than they really did. There are probably genes involved other than those for blue eyes and brown eyes only. Maybe other genes at other places in the chromosomes are also involved. We all know, for instance, that there are eyes of intermediate color. There are light-brown eyes, blue eyes with flecks of brown in them, greenish-blue eyes, and grayish-blue eyes.

All this complicates eye-color inheritance.

The other physical characteristics we mentioned in Chapter 3 have even more complicated relations to the genes. A man's height, the shape of his skull, the color of his skin, all the physical characteristics that have been most commonly used in determining race, involve, in all likelihood, more than one gene series.

Scientists did not discover the rules of inheritance by observing human beings. That would have been too complicated. Instead, the science of genetics got its start with an Austrian monk named Gregor Johann Mendel, whose hobby was cultivating plants in the monastery garden. In particular, he carried on experiments with different varieties of pea plants. (This was about a hundred years ago.)

There are several advantages to working with pea plants. Being plants, they do not run around or fight with one another or present special feeding problems. Furthermore, they can be *crossed* in whatever way the experimenter wishes. That is, he can take *pollen* from the blossom of one pea plant and place it on the *pistil* of the blossom of another pea plant. The pollen contains cells similar to the sperm cells in animals; the pistil contains cells similar to the egg cells in animals. By crossing plants, he gets a fertilized ovum which develops first into a seed (which is a pea in the case of a pea plant) and then, when the seed is planted, into a new plant.

An advantage of the pea plant in particular is that it possesses several conspicuous characteristics each of which is controlled by two genes of a single gene series. (Mendel did not know this, of course. This was simply his good fortune.)

The pea plant has a place on a pair of chromosomes, for instance, for a gene which we might call the seed-form gene series. If the plant possesses one gene of such a series, the peas produced by the plant are smooth and round. Let's call that the smooth-pea gene. If the plant possesses a second gene of that series instead, the peas it produces are angular and wrinkled. Let's call that the wrinkled-pea gene.

Now Mendel found that, if he crossed a plant of

the smooth-pea type with another of the same kind, all the peas produced were smooth. If he crossed two plants of the wrinkled-pea type, all the peas produced were wrinkled. That, of course, wouldn't surprise anyone.

However, when he crossed a smooth-pea plant with a wrinkled-pea plant, the peas produced were all smooth. There were no wrinkled peas at all. (He had discovered that the smooth-pea gene was dominant over the wrinkled-pea gene.)

Furthermore, when Mendel crossed the mixed type with itself, he found that the peas produced were mostly smooth. A certain proportion of the peas, however, were wrinkled. (He had discovered that a recessive gene might seem completely drowned out, yet would appear as good as new in the next generation.)

Mendel noted down all these facts and many more. He wrote a description of his experiments and had it printed in a scientific journal. This was in 1866. Unfortunately, no one paid much attention to it at the time. The scientific journal was a small one, and experiments with pea plants didn't seem to be very exciting.

However, over thirty years later, after Mendel was dead, other scientists, who were interested in the mechanics of inheritance, discovered his reports. They realized at once that this obscure man had already done all the fundamental work.

It is very pleasant to be able to say that the dead Austrian monk was instantly given the credit he deserved. To this day the rules that govern the inheritance of physical characteristics are referred to as *Mendel's Laws*.

THE ODDS OF THREE TO ONE

Just above we said that pea plants of mixed smooth-wrinkled heritage, when crossed with each other, produced mostly smooth peas, but also some wrinkled peas. Is there any way of deciding how much of each variety will be formed?

The answer is yes. To explain that answer, let us go back to the genes.

Plant cells, like animal cells, have chromosomes and genes. Pea plants that arise as a result of a cross between the wrinkled-pea variety and the smooth-pea variety have both genes of the seed-form gene series in their cells. The wrinkled-pea gene (let's call it W) is on one particular chromosome, and the smooth-pea gene (let's call it S) is on the twin of that chromosome. Such a plant is heterozygous. Every cell contains both S and W.

The pea plant produces cells which are equivalent to the egg cells of animals and other cells which are equivalent to the sperm cells. (Let's call them simply female cells and male cells.) Both types are produced by maturation divisions in which the pairs of chromosomes split up. As in human beings, one of each pair of chromosomes enters one cell while the other member of the pair enters the second cell.

When a reproductive cell of the heterozygous SW variety undergoes maturation, the S gene is carried by one chromosome into one cell, and the W gene is carried by the other chromosome into the second cell. The result is that there are two types of female cells produced in equal quantities, one containing S and one containing W. The same is true of the male cells.

Now suppose we allow an SW variety of pea plant to fertilize itself. Four different kinds of fertilization may take place. A male cell containing S may fertilize a female cell containing S; a male cell containing S may fertilize a female cell containing W; a male cell containing W may fertilize a female cell containing S; a male cell containing W may fertilize a female cell containing W.

We can make a little table of what happens, as follows:

Male Cell	Female Cell	Fertilized Cell	Phenotype
S	S	SS	Smooth
S	W	SW	Smooth
W	S	WS	Smooth
W	W	WW	Wrinkled

Notice that an SW or a WS variety produces smooth peas because S is dominant over W.

Now any one of the four cases can happen. There is no reason why one type of fertilization should take place more often than another. The result is that, in the long run, the four types of fertilization take place in equal numbers. Three of them, however, give rise to smooth peas and only one to wrinkled peas. It is a general rule, for that reason, that when heterozygous plants are crossed with one another, the dominant characteristic occurs three times as often as the recessive one. In the case we are discussing, three smooth peas are produced for every wrinkled pea. The odds in favor of smooth peas are three to one.

Sometimes it happens that neither of two genes of a particular series is truly dominant. For instance, there is a flower called the four o'clock, which exists in several varieties. One type has red blossoms, another white. When the red type and the white are crossed, the resulting plants have pink blossoms. This is called *incomplete dominance.* (Incomplete dominance often occurs in human characteristics and helps to complicate matters.)

When the pink four o'clocks are crossed with one another, the four possible combinations of red-blossom genes (R) and white-blossom genes (W) are RR, RW, WR, and WW. The resulting plants include those with red blossoms, pink blossoms, and white blossoms. Since there is one combination which will give red blossoms (RR) and one which will give white (WW), these will be produced in equal quantities. There are two combinations which will give pink (RW and WR); so there will be twice as many pink blossoms as either reds or whites.

THE DISADVANTAGE OF SMALL NUMBERS

All sorts of similar problems can be solved by working out the different gene combinations. We can solve them without ever seeing a pea plant. Mendel, however, was not so fortunate. He never heard of genes and gene series. When he crossed different types of pea plants, he had to count every one of the thousands of peas produced and sort them into the various characteristics in order to find out what happened.

But there is an advantage in large numbers. The question which gene will join which during fertilization is a matter of chance, like the tossing of a coin. Now in coin-tossing we all know that there is an even chance that a coin will turn up heads. In the long run, almost exactly half of your throws will end up heads. A few tails more or less won't matter if the total number of throws is large, but will matter if it is small. If you throw the coin twice, you may get no heads. Even if you throw the coin ten times, you may get no heads. With hundreds or thousands of tosses, however, it becomes more and more likely that the heads and tails will even up.

The same goes for the three-to-one odds in favor of the dominant. A thousand peas resulting from crossing heterozygous pea plants might yield 742 smooth peas and 258 wrinkled peas. That isn't exactly 3 to 1, but with such large numbers, ending up with eight or ten, too many smooth peas or too few smooth peas don't matter. It's still very close to 3 to 1. In fact, crosses such as this always work out to give results that are close to what you would expect by considering the possible gene combinations. This is strong evidence that the gene theory is correct. You wouldn't expect a wrong theory to work out so neatly.

But what if every crossing produced only a few offspring, as with human beings? Suppose two parents heterozygous for brown eyes had four children. Would we expect exactly three to have brown eyes (the dominant characteristic) and one blue eyes? Not necessarily. The number is too small. We can't rely on Mendel's Laws to work perfectly in small numbers, just as we can't be sure that four tosses of a coin will always produce two heads and two tails.

From heterozygous brown-eyed parents, any combination of brown-eyed and blue-eyed children can result. The combination of three brown eyes and one blue eye is most likely and would occur almost half the time. Other combinations, however, would also occur.

For instance, if you had the records of 256 cases in which heterozygous parents had four children each, you might find that in 108 cases there were three brown-eyed children and one blue-eyed child. In 81 cases, however, all four children might be brown-eyed. In 54 cases, two might be brown-eyed and two blue-eyed. In 12 cases, one might be brown-eyed and three blue-eyed. In 1 case, all four might be blue-eyed.

The numbers given above are worked out by using a branch of mathematics called *probability*. It deals with problems that involve chance happenings, such as the results of coin-tossing. Since the answer to the question "Which sperm cell fertilizes which egg cell?" depends, as we have seen, upon chance, probability is much used in the science of genetics.

GENES IN THE PLURAL

Now let's consider two gene series, each with its own set of genes. There are two possibilities: the two genes might be on different chromosomes, or they might be in different places on the same chromosome.

Suppose they are on two different chromosomes. A case like that is found in Mendel's peas. In addition to the seed-form gene series with its smooth-pea gene and wrinkled-pea gene, there is also a seed-color gene series. The seed-color gene series also includes two kinds of genes. One of these causes the peas formed to be yellow (a yellow-pea gene), and the other causes them to be green (a green-pea gene). The yellow-pea gene is dominant over the green-pea gene.

If we take a pea plant which produces smooth green peas and cross it with a plant which produces wrinkled yellow peas, all the peas produced as a result will be smooth and yellow. Both the smoothness and the yellowness are dominant. The plants grown from these peas, however, will be heterozygous in both respects. They will contain the wrinkled-pea gene of the seed-form gene series and the green-pea gene of the seed-color gene series. These recessive genes aren't visible, but they are there just the same, and will show up in future offspring.

When these heterozygous plants form female cells and male cells, the chromosomes separate as usual. Which chromosome of each pair goes to which end of the cell is purely chance. One female cell may end up with the wrinkled-pea and yellow-pea genes, one with the smooth-pea and green-pea genes, one with the wrinkled-pea and green-pea genes, and one with the smooth-pea and yellow-pea genes. The same thing happens with the male cells.

When heterozygous plants are crossed with one another, any combination of male and female cells may take place. The result is that all sorts of peas are formed. It is even possible to figure out the numbers of each kind that would be formed. If we list the ways in which the male cells and female cells might combine, it turns out that, of every 16 peas formed, 9 would be smooth and yellow, 3 would be smooth and green, 3 would be wrinkled and yellow, and 1 would be wrinkled and green.

When two or more different characteristics are passed along from parents to offspring in all possible combinations, they are said to show *independent assortment*.

But what if the seed-form gene and the seed-color gene had been on the same chromosome?

Suppose the smooth-pea gene of one gene series and the yellow-pea gene of the other gene series were on one chromosome of a heterozygous plant. The wrinkled-pea and green-pea genes of those gene series would be on the twin of that chromosome. During maturation, when the chromosomes divide, the yellow-pea gene would always go with the smooth-pea gene for they are on the same chromosome. For the same reason the wrinkled-pea gene would always go with the green-pea gene. If that were so, the peas from a cross of heterozygous plants would always be either smooth and yellow or wrinkled and green. There would ordinarily be no peas that would be smooth and green or wrinkled and yellow.

When two characteristics are always or almost always inherited together, one can suspect that their genes are located on the same chromosome. Such characteristics are said to be *linked characteristics*. Attempts have been made to determine what human characteristics may be linked in this fashion, but the situation is very complicated, and not much has yet been accomplished.

There is one type of linkage of an entirely different sort, however, which is known to occur in plants and animals (and in human beings, too). We will take that up next.

THE Y-CHROMOSOME AGAIN

You may remember that we said that men and women have different chromosome arrangements. Women have twenty-four perfect pairs of chromosomes, including two X-chromosomes. Men have twenty-three perfect pairs and one imperfect pair. The imperfect pair consists of an X-chromosome and the stunted Y-chromosome. The Y-chromosome carries few, if any, genes, and this is the source of much trouble for the male sex.

A gene located on the twenty-fourth pair of chromosomes controls the ability of the human eye to tell the difference between the colors red and green. An imperfect gene belonging to the same gene-series is unable to manage this type of color vision. When this imperfect gene is the only one a human being possesses, he cannot differentiate red and green. He is *colorblind*. Let us call the normal gene N and the color-blind gene C.

A man who is color-blind possesses the C gene on one chromosome of his twenty-fourth pair. If he had a normal gene as well, all would be fine; but he hasn't. The other chromosome of the twenty-fourth pair is the Y-chromosome, which has no gene of that gene series at all. Let's call the Y-chromosome Y for short. The gene combination of a color-blind man is therefore CY.

Our color-blind man will develop two kinds of sperm cells. One will get the normal twenty-fourth chromosome carrying the color-blind gene. That will be a C sperm cell. The other will get the Y-chromosome without any color-vision gene at all. That will be a Y sperm cell. Both sperm cells will be formed in equal numbers, of course.

Next, we will suppose that the man is married to a woman with normal color vision. Both chromosomes of her twenty-fourth pair have the normal gene; so she is NN. All her egg cells are the same in this respect. All have a normal gene and are N egg cells.

What kinds of fertilized ova are formed? Either a C sperm cell fertilizes an N egg cell, or a Y sperm cell fertilizes an N egg cell. The fertilized ova are all either NC or NY.

You may remember from a previous chapter that a fertilized egg cell containing a Y-chromosome always develops into a male. All the NY fertilized ova develop into boys. We see, then, that when a color-blind husband has sons by a normal wife, they are all normal. None of them have the color-blind gene at all; so color-blindness will not necessarily appear among their descendants.

When a fertilized egg cell does not have a Y-chromosome, it always develops into a female. All the NC children are therefore girls, and all the girls are heterozygous. Fortunately, the normal gene is dominant over the color-blind gene. For that reason the daughters born to a color-blind man and a normal woman can see color perfectly well. However, unlike

SEX-LINKED INHERITANCE
CASE I

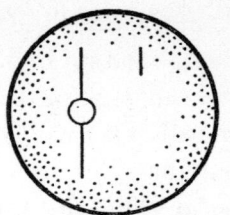

COLOR-BLIND FATHER
(ONE GENE FOR COLOR-BLINDNESS AND ONE Y-CHROMOSOME)

SPERM CELLS, HALF WITH GENE FOR COLOR-BLINDNESS AND HALF WITH Y-CHROMOSOME

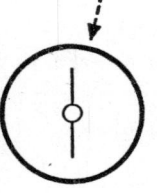 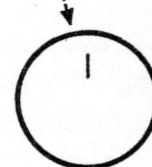

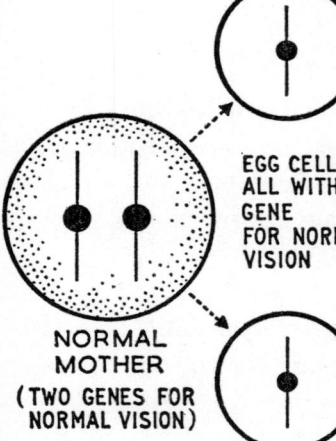

EGG CELLS, ALL WITH GENE FOR NORMAL VISION

NORMAL MOTHER
(TWO GENES FOR NORMAL VISION)

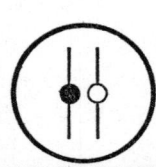 DAUGHTER WITH NORMAL VISION, BUT CARRYING GENE FOR COLOR-BLINDNESS

 SON WITH NORMAL VISION; NO GENE FOR COLOR-BLINDNESS

 DAUGHTER WITH NORMAL VISION, BUT CARRYING GENE FOR COLOR-BLINDNESS

 SON WITH NORMAL VISION; NO GENE FOR COLOR-BLINDNESS

SEX-LINKED INHERITANCE CASE 2

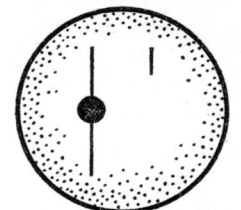

NORMAL FATHER
(ONE GENE FOR NORMAL VISION
AND ONE Y-CHROMOSOME)

SPERM CELLS, HALF WITH
A GENE FOR NORMAL VISION,
HALF WITH A Y-CHROMOSOME

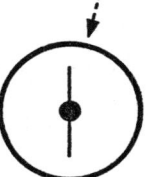 

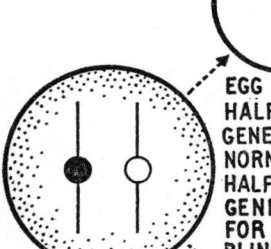

MOTHER
WITH NORMAL
VISION BUT
CARRYING
ONE GENE FOR
COLOR-BLINDNESS
AS RECESSIVE

EGG CELLS,
HALF WITH
GENE FOR
NORMAL VISION,
HALF WITH
GENE
FOR COLOR-
BLINDNESS

NORMAL
DAUGHTER,
NO GENE FOR
COLOR-
BLINDNESS

NORMAL SON,
NO GENE FOR
COLOR-
BLINDNESS

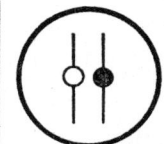

DAUGHTER WITH
NORMAL VISION,
BUT CARRYING
ONE GENE FOR
COLOR-BLINDNESS
AS RECESSIVE

COLOR-BLIND
SON

the sons of the marriage, the daughters possess the color-blind gene and can pass it along to their children.

Suppose, for instance, that one of these heterozygous girls (NC) eventually marries a normal male with one good color-vision gene and, of course, one Y-chromosome (NY). What happens? The girl produces two types of egg cells, one N and one C, equal in number. The man produces two types of sperm cells, one N and one Y, equal in number.

The possible fertilized ova will then be NN, NC, NY, and CY. The daughters of this marriage will be without the Y-chromosome. They will be either NN or NC. The NN girls are perfectly normal. The NC girls see color perfectly, too, but they are heterozygous. They carry the color-blind gene.

The boys of this marriage will have the Y-chromosome. They will be either NY or CY. The NY boys are perfectly normal. The CY boys are color-blind.

This sort of thing can be continued from generation to generation. It will always be the boy who is color-blind and practically never the girl. However, it is the girl who transmits color-blindness, and not the boy.

It is possible, of course, for a girl to be color-blind also if she happens to have two color-blind genes (CC). This can happen if a color-blind man marries a woman whose father was color-blind and who is carrying the color-blind gene. Then there is a fifty-fifty chance that a girl born of this marriage will be color-blind. Such cases are known, but they are very rare. (All the sons of a color-blind woman will be color-blind, no matter whom she marries. See if you can figure that out for yourself.)

Whenever a characteristic, like color-blindness, seems to occur in only one sex and not in the other, it is said to be *sex-linked*.

Another sex-linked characteristic you may have heard of is *hemophilia*. This is a condition in which the blood, for some reason, refuses to clot. Even a minor cut can be fatal to a person suffering from this disease, for without special treatment he just bleeds and bleeds.

Hemophilia is inherited in the same way as color-blindness. With very rare exceptions it is only men who have it, but it is the women who transmit it.

One interesting thing about hemophilia is that Queen Victoria of England may have been heterozygous in this respect. Since the normal blood-clotting gene is dominant over the hemophilia gene, we can't be certain. Her blood clotted normally. However, hemophilia cropped up in certain of her male descendants. The oldest son of Tsar Nicholas II of Russia (whose wife was one of Victoria's daughters) had hemophilia. So did the oldest son of King Alfonso XIII of Spain (whose wife was one of Victoria's granddaughters). We'll have occasion to mention Victoria again in the next chapter.

7

Rules Can Be Broken

LOCATING THE GENE

THE RULES OF INHERITANCE, as described in previous chapters, certainly seem to be simple and clean-cut. But inheritance doesn't always follow the rules.

Let us consider once again the case of linked genes. You may remember that linked genes are located on the same chromosome and should, therefore, always be inherited together. Notice that we say "should be."

Suppose that in men the gene for hair color and the gene for eye color are linked—that is, that they occur on the same chromosome. And suppose, moreover, that both the father and the mother of a certain family are heterozygous in both hair color and eye color. That means that each possesses a chromosome carrying, let us say, a gene for brown hair and a gene for brown eyes. Each also possesses the twin of that chromosome, carrying a gene for blond hair and a gene for blue eyes. Blond hair and blue eyes are both recessive; so both parents have brown hair and brown eyes.

Some of the offspring of such a marriage may inherit two chromosomes both carrying the gene for blond hair. These have blond hair. But, if they inherit these two chromosomes, they receive not only two

LOCATING THE GENE

genes for blond hair but also two genes for blue eyes. The children that have blond hair also have blue eyes. Those that are brown-haired are also brown-eyed. No children are born with blond hair and brown eyes or with brown hair and blue eyes in this particular family.

That is as it "should be" but not as it *is*. In a family such as we have just described, a child with brown hair and blue eyes might be born, or one with blond hair and brown eyes.

But how can that be? How can genes on the same chromosome be inherited separately?

When chromosomes are lined up, previous to separation, each chromosome is lying immediately next to its twin. Sometimes it is even twisted about its twin. At this point *crossing over* may take place; that is, the two paired chromosomes may exchange bits of their substance. In this way a chromosome carrying a gene for blond hair and one for blue eyes may exchange

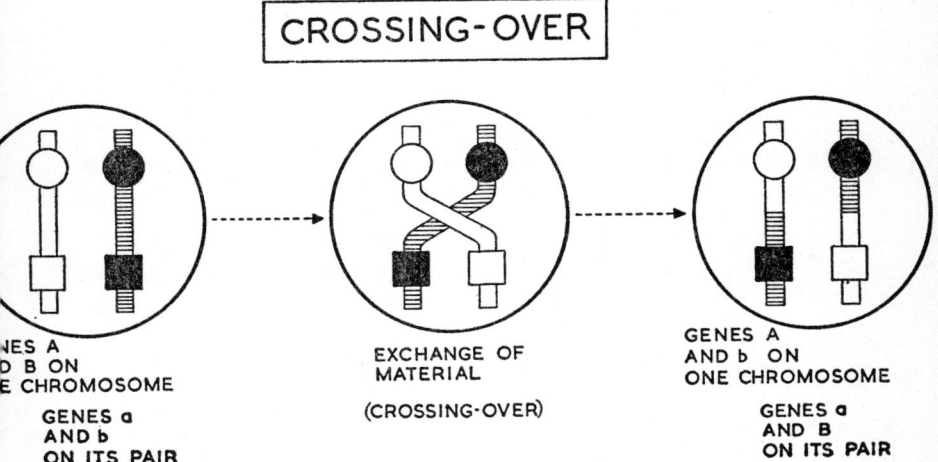

CROSSING-OVER

GENES A AND B ON ONE CHROMOSOME
GENES a AND b ON ITS PAIR

EXCHANGE OF MATERIAL
(CROSSING-OVER)

GENES A AND b ON ONE CHROMOSOME
GENES a AND B ON ITS PAIR

the part containing the gene for blond hair with its twin, receiving in exchange a part containing a gene for brown hair. An egg cell or sperm cell may then be formed which will carry the genes for brown hair and blue eyes or for blond hair and brown eyes.

It is difficult to tell which genes are linked in human chromosomes and when crossing over takes place. For one thing, human beings have twenty-four pairs of chromosomes, which is a large number to handle. In addition, a human family includes only a few children, often not more than one or two. It is always difficult and sometimes impossible to decide questions of genetics when only small numbers of individuals are concerned. Although we used them as an example, it isn't really known whether hair color and eye color are linked in man.

We know more about the genes of a small insect named *Drosophila*, which has turned out to be very useful to geneticists. This fruit-fly has numerous genes which affect the nature of its eyes or wings in a variety of easily observed ways. It has only four pairs of chromosomes for these genes to be distributed over. Furthermore, *Drosophila* can breed ten times a year and produce a hundred young at each breeding. With few chromosomes and many offspring to consider, it is not difficult to determine which genes are linked in *Drosophila* and to observe crossing over when it occurs.

Suppose that two genes are on the same chromosome and very close together. If a piece of chromosome containing one of those genes is exchanged during crossing over, it is very likely to contain the other gene, too. If the two genes are fairly far apart, it may often happen that a piece of chromosome containing one of the genes is exchanged while the piece containing the other remains behind. We can, in fact, make a general rule: the farther apart two genes are on a chromosome, the more likely they are to be separated during crossing over.

Crossing over has been so thoroughly studied in *Drosophila* that for almost every two linked genes it is known how often crossing over separates them. In this way the distances between all the genes can be calculated. Using that calculation, one can even decide where the different genes must occur on each chromosome.

Elaborate *chromosome maps* have in this way been drawn up for *Drosophila*. Over a hundred different genes have been accurately located on one or another of its four pairs of chromosomes. It is one of the triumphs of genetics that genes, which have never actually been seen by the scientists who study them, can be pinpointed in this fashion just by studying the manner in which they are inherited.

THE OUTSIDE INFLUENCES

Genes don't exist in a vacuum. They may control physical characteristics, but sometimes they are not the only control.

There are several genes, for instance, that influence the skin color of a man. Two men who have identical sets of these genes should have the same skin color. If one of those men is an office worker and the other a farmer, however, their skin color may well be different despite the genes. The office worker will be pale, and the farmer, continually exposed to wind and sun, will be darker.

In this way the *external environment* (that is, the world existing outside the body) can affect the action of a gene. Such changes caused by the environment confuse us, of course, and make it more difficult to divide mankind into races on the basis of physical characteristics.

A person's height is influenced by several genes. It is also influenced by diet. A man's genes may be of a type which ought to make him six feet tall by the time he reaches full growth. Yet if, in childhood, he hasn't enough to eat, and if, in particular, he does not get enough of the bone-making minerals, he may end up only five and a half feet in height.

American-born children of European immigrants often grow to be taller than their parents. American air hasn't changed their genes. It is just that their diet in America is usually better than their parents' diet had been in Europe. Even within America there has been an increase in height in the last century. The soldiers of the American army in World War II averaged an inch taller than the soldiers of the American army in World War I. This is probably due to improved infant nutrition rather than to any change in genes.

Then, too, one gene may have an unexpected effect upon another.

We are all acquainted with the physical characteristic called baldness. We all know that it is an inherited characteristic. If your father is bald, and you are male, you may become bald as you grow older—provided you have inherited the proper genes.

Now chemicals produced by certain cells in the

body have an effect on baldness. The chemicals are called *androgens*.* Females produce them in small quantities, males in somewhat larger quantities.

Some scientists have come to the conclusion that baldness is more likely to take place when a person's body contains large quantities of androgens. It is for this reason, they think, that men frequently get bald while women rarely do.

Now suppose a boy inherits his father's gene for baldness, but also inherits a gene which brings about the production of somewhat less androgen than his father produced. The effect of the gene for baldness may be lost. The boy may keep his hair as he grows older.

In this way, one gene can mask the action of a second gene. The simple rules of genetics do not seem to apply. The effect of one gene upon another is hard to study in man, and easier to study in a creature such as *Drosophila*.

THE SUDDEN CHANGE

There is a still more remarkable way in which the inheritance of physical characteristics may differ from what is ordinarily expected.

In the previous chapter, you may remember, we said that Queen Victoria of England probably carried

---

* Androgens belong to a class of chemicals known as *hormones*. The effect of androgens on baldness is one of their less important properties. The most important function of the androgens is their control of the changes that take place in a boy as he enters his teens. They regulate the deepening of his voice, the growth of hair on his face and other parts of his body, and so on. For that reason, the androgens are also called the *male sex hormones*. There are also *female sex hormones*, which are called *estrogens*.

the gene for hemophilia since it showed up in some of her male descendants. But, if that is so, where did Victoria get the gene? As far as we know, there were no cases of hemophilia among her ancestors.

One conclusion is that the gene originated in Victoria.

But how can a new gene be originated when all the genes are inherited from the two parents?

You may remember that at the metaphase, in the process of cell division, every one of the forty-eight chromosomes autoreproduces. That is, each brings about the formation of another chromosome exactly like itself, with all genes like its own. Every once in a while, however, the machinery slips up. Something (we are not always quite sure what) goes wrong, and a chromosome is produced which is not quite identical with the one that is used as a pattern. Perhaps one gene has been imperfectly reproduced and works differently or doesn't work at all.

When this happens, the daughter cell that receives this chromosome with the changed gene is not quite the same chemically as its parent cell. All the new cells produced from this daughter cell are different from the original parent cell, since at each cell division the changed chromosome reproduces itself. It does not change back to the original chromosome.

Whenever a chromosome reproduces itself imperfectly, so that there is some sudden change in the chemistry of the daughter cell, we call the process a *mutation*. (Even a change in a single gene can produce very noticeable results. Some scientists think that can-

THE SUDDEN CHANGE

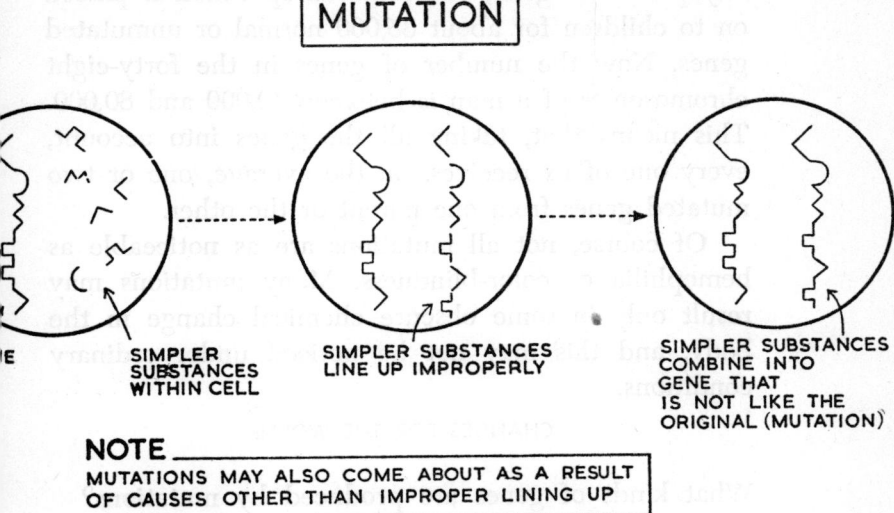

cer cells may arise from normal cells as a result of a mutation.)

Occasionally a mutation occurs among the cells which eventually gives rise to sperm cells or egg cells. When that happens, at least some of the sperm cells or egg cells that are later produced contain the changed gene. Offspring resulting from these will show characteristics that seem completely new and seem not to have been inherited at all.

How often does this happen? How often is a mutated gene passed on from parents to children?

This problem has been investigated for a number of different types of mutations in man, and the answer seems to come out about the same for each type. For any particular gene, one mutated specimen is passed on to children for about 35,000 normal or unmutated genes. Now the number of genes in the forty-eight chromosomes of a man is between 40,000 and 80,000. This means that, taking all the genes into account, every one of us receives, on the average, one or two mutated genes from one parent or the other.

Of course, not all mutations are as noticeable as hemophilia or color-blindness. Many mutations may result only in some obscure chemical change in the body, and this may not be noticed under ordinary conditions.

CHANGES FOR THE WORSE

What kinds of genes are produced by mutations?

Well, suppose you had a blueprint of a very complex machine and all the structural materials necessary to build one by following the blueprint. Then suppose that at some point, through some mistake, you bolted some particular part into the wrong place. Without noticing that, you continued until you were finished. Would your machine work properly? You know that the chances are that it wouldn't. With one part in the wrong place, the whole thing would probably be completely useless.

For similar reasons, a mutated gene is almost sure to perform its function more poorly than the normal gene. Perhaps it might not perform its function at all. In general, then, most mutations are for the worse.

There is no way of predicting exactly when a mutation will occur or what kind of mutation it will be when it does occur. Geneticists have to study mutations as they happen and must take what they get. One thing they can do, though (at least when they're working with plants, animals and bacteria), is to increase the number of mutations. In that way they have more cases to study and choose from.

The easiest way to increase the number of mutations is to expose creatures to certain kinds of radiation—for example, *X-rays*. These X-rays bombard the genes and occasionally upset the atom arrangements within them. This changes the chemical nature of the genes. A gene is mutated and gives rise to further mutated genes during autoreproduction.

This sort of thing is one of the serious dangers of the atom and hydrogen bombs, perhaps the most serious danger. Whenever such a bomb explodes, a vast flood of *gamma rays* are formed and sent out in all directions. Gamma rays are even more likely to cause mutations than are X-rays. People who are far enough away from the explosion to survive the heat and blast may still be riddled by so many gamma rays (which are unseen and unfelt) as to be in great danger. The gamma rays can cause enough chemical changes in the genes and in other body substances to upset the workings of the body completely and to kill it in a few days, weeks, or months, depending on the dose.

Furthermore, the products of atomic explosions circulate through the atmosphere and the oceans and produce small but steady amounts of gamma rays and other kinds of radiation. These may not be enough to kill anyone, but they may increase the number of mutations in human beings. Since most mutations are for the worse, there could be a general weakening of human vitality and efficiency over all the world regardless of where the atom bombs are exploded.

But, if mutations are always taking place, why haven't human vitality and efficiency declined to zero long ago?

We must remember that mutated genes don't last as well as normal genes do. A man with hemophilia, for instance, may bleed to death as a result of some small wound. He is much more likely to die young than is a man with normal blood. He is not likely to live long enough to marry and have children. There is thus less chance of passing on a hemophilia gene than of passing on a normal one. The hemophilia gene has less *survival value*.

The same may be said for other mutated genes. Albinos are more seriously affected by the sun and have weak eyes. People who inherit mutated genes that result in chemical disorders of the body don't utilize their foodstuffs efficiently; they die sooner and have fewer children unless they receive special care.

Under natural conditions, mutations for the worse remain unimportant. The mutated genes die out as fast as they are produced. In our highly civilized state, however, mutations for the worse may accumulate as the result of efficient medical care. They may also be produced at a faster rate as a result of atomic explosions. Some geneticists are quite concerned for the future because of these possibilities.

CHANGES FOR THE BETTER

Once in a long while a mutation may benefit an organism. It may help the organism live longer or more efficiently in the particular environment it is in. You can see, for example, that any mutation that enabled a rabbit to run faster would help that rabbit escape its enemies. It would have a good chance of living longer than rabbits without the mutation. It would have time to produce more than the average number of litters. Some of its descendants would possess this "extra speed" gene, and they would live longer and produce more young. Before very long the new mutated rabbits would have completely replaced the old stock.

The same thing would happen if a mutated gene caused a lion to have stronger muscles or a dog to have a keener sense of smell.

A mutation can be beneficial under one set of circumstances and not under another. Consider the ancestors of mankind as they existed tens of thousands of years ago. We have no way of being sure of the color of the skins of these ancestors. Let us suppose the skins were of some intermediate color, not very dark and not very light.

Now let us suppose that occasionally a mutation changed the skin-color genes in such a way that increased amounts of melanin were formed. The skin color of such mutated individuals would be very dark. If this took place in tropical lands like Africa or India or the East Indies, such dark, mutated individuals would be able to withstand the sun better. Their skin pigmentation would protect them. They could work more efficiently and perhaps have more opportunity to have and to support children. The black-skin mutation would spread and spread and finally take over.

Suppose, instead, that a mutation caused the skin-color genes to form very little melanin. Such mutated individuals would be very light. If they happened to be living in northern lands, their light skin would be more transparent to the weak northern sun. The weak sunlight would be better able to form vitamin D in the skins of such people. Their children would be less likely to have rickets (a bone disease brought about by a shortage of vitamin D) and would therefore be stronger. Pretty soon that mutation would spread and take over.

A dark-skin mutation in Norway, on the other hand, wouldn't succeed. Nor would a light-skin mutation in the Congo. A mutation is for the better or for the worse as it fits or unfits the organism for its particular surroundings.

The way in which mutations endure or die out according to their usefulness under particular circumstances is known as *natural selection*. As a result of natural selection, creatures tend to *adapt* themselves to their environment—that is, to fit in with it well.

The dark skin of a Negro is an *adaptation*. So, probably, is the fact that he has a richer supply of sweat glands than other groups of people have, since it allows him to keep cool more efficiently. The Negro's nose is flat and broad-nostriled, perhaps for easier breathing in a hot, humid atmosphere. His hair forms tight curls covering his head like a skullcap and may protect it from the direct rays of the sun and consequent sunstroke.

The thin, high-bridged nose of the European is also an adaptation. During the winter the air he breathes travels through a long passage and is warmed up and moistened before entering the lungs.

You may say, "If this is so, why aren't Eskimos as pale-skinned as Norwegians? Why don't the Indians of tropical America have the same coloring and nose-type as the Negroes of tropical Africa?"

You must remember that mutations happen hit-or-miss, by chance. Certain mutations might be useful if they were to happen; but if they don't happen, they have no chance to be useful. In the long run, the long, long run, the chances are good that all kinds of mutations will happen and that all sorts of changes for the better will take place.

You may think that this long, long run we talk about is very time-consuming, and it is. You may think that hit-or-miss is not an efficient way to get things done, and it isn't. But, remember, life has existed on the earth a long time. The first living cells were developed over a billion years ago, and ever since then life has been slowly changing and adjusting itself to various environments.

Tremendous groups of animals have flourished for hundreds of millions of years and then died out because they couldn't adapt themselves to a changing environment. (Remember, as the earth's climate changes, the kinds of surrounding animals change. The environment is always changing. Perhaps the change isn't noticeable over a few thousand years, but it can be pretty noticeable over a hundred thousand or a million years.)

The process whereby mutations gradually change creatures over hundreds of millions of years, forming fish that are perfectly at home in the ocean, birds in the air, lizards in the desert, chamois in the mountains, squirrels in the trees, and so on, is known as *evolution*.

Scientists study the progress of evolution by considering remnants of animals of long ages ago which have been preserved in the rocks. These remnants may be bones or shells, impressions of an animal's body against mud which later hardened, sometimes even merely footprints. (Such remnants are called *fossil remains*.)

By studying fossil remains, scientists have been able to follow the path of evolution of some creatures, such as the horse and the elephant. They have even puzzled out some of the facts concerning the evolution of man.

They have found fossils of man-like creatures that existed between twenty thousand and a million years ago. Their brains are smaller than those of modern man but larger than those of apes. Their jaws are larger and stronger than those of modern man and their teeth bigger. They don't stand as erect. These fossils are frequently given names according to the places where they were found, such as Java Man, Peking Man, Rhodesian Man, Neanderthal Man.

The exact line of descent of modern man is not yet known. It does seem, however, that all races of modern man have the same line of descent, which is why they form a single species. And since modern man developed, about fifty thousand years ago or less, there has not yet been time for the forces of evolution to make more than a few minor changes between the different groups of human beings.

8

The Telltale Blood

RACE, BY WAY OF GENES

AT THE VERY BEGINNING of this book, we said that a race is a group of people who resemble one another more than they resemble outsiders. We tried to show that resemblances in cultural characteristics, such as language, clothing, and feeding habits, don't count. That left us with resemblances in physical characteristics.

Then we explained how your physical characteristics are controlled by the genes you inherit. People with similar genes will have similar physical characteristics. They will resemble one another.

But how can we tell whether two persons have similar genes? We can't see the genes, and even if we could, we couldn't tell one gene from another just by looking at them. We couldn't tell whether a particular gene was for blue eyes or for brown eyes. We can tell the nature of a gene only by looking at a human being and seeing what it does to him. This takes us right back to physical characteristics.

But we don't want to get back to just any physical characteristic. We can't make use of genes by themselves, true, but neither can we make use of physical characteristics by themselves. We need both. We need a physical characteristic for which we know the exact gene background. Then we can understand exactly how the physical characteristic is inherited, how it spreads among the population, and how it can be used to divide mankind into races.

Well, which physical characteristics can we use then? By a stroke of poor luck, none of the physical characteristics which seem most obvious to us are very well understood in terms of genes. Skull shape, height, and skin color are all probably dependent on more than one gene series. We don't know how many, and we don't know what kind of genes each gene series has. So we don't really know exactly how such characteristics are inherited. What's more, these physical characteristics are determined not only by the genes but also by environment.

What we really need is some characteristic which is decided by a single gene series with known genes—a characteristic, moreover, which is decided only by the gene and is not modified by the environment.

Where do we find such a characteristic?

One answer is: in blood.

THE DIFFERENCES IN BLOOD

It is quite common to hear people talk of blood as though it differed according to race or nationality. You may have heard talk of "Negro blood" or "French blood" or even "Jones blood" or "Smith blood." During World War II some people wanted the American Red Cross to keep the blood it received from white people separate from that which it received from Negroes.

Supposedly this was to keep white soldiers from receiving transfusions of "Negro blood."

Actually, this is nonsense and superstition. If a scientist or a doctor were given a sample of normal blood, there would be no way in the world he could determine for sure whether it came from a man or a woman, a Frenchman or a German, a Negro, an Aboriginal, a Chinese, or an American. Nor could your body, if the blood were put into your veins.

Yet there are ways in which your blood may be different from your neighbor's, or even from the blood of your closest relatives. Let us see how.

Every once in a while, during an operation or as a result of a serious wound, a man or woman may suffer considerable loss of blood. To keep the patient alive, it is sometimes necessary, then, to transfer blood into his body from that of some healthy person (called a *donor*) who is willing to give his or her blood for the purpose. (A person in normal health can easily give up a pint of blood without pain or any harmful effect. The body quickly manufactures new blood to replace that much.)

Such a transfer of blood is called a *transfusion*.

When a patient needs a quick transfusion of blood, it is not enough just to grab any healthy person as the donor. The blood of one donor may save the patient's life. The blood of another, equally strong and healthy, may kill the patient. The use of a relative as a blood donor is no insurance. The blood of the patient's own mother or sister may be deadly, while the blood of a complete stranger, of a foreigner, or of a member of a different race, may be life-saving.

Why is this so? Let's consider blood a bit more closely.

The liquid portion of blood is called *plasma*. Plasma is mostly water, but it contains many dissolved substances of great importance to body chemistry. Floating in the plasma are various kinds of cells. The most numerous of these cells are the *red cells*, which are also called *erythrocytes*. These are very small and simple cells. They are so simple that they do not even contain nuclei. The erythrocytes are the only human cells which do not contain nuclei.

The erythrocytes do contain small quantities of certain chemicals known as *blood-group substances*. Two important kinds of blood-group substances are referred to simply as A and B. In any one person, all the erythrocytes are alike in the kind of blood-group substances they contain. In one case, perhaps, all the erythrocytes contain A, and none of them contain B. A person with such erythrocytes is said to possess *blood type A*.

In the plasma of a person of blood type A there is dissolved a substance which has no effect on A. However, if that substance in the plasma were to come in contact with erythrocytes containing B, it would combine with those erythrocytes and make them clump together in one large sticky mess. The substance in the plasma is therefore called *anti-B*. Anti-B is said to *agglutinate* erythrocytes containing B.

On the other hand, a person of *blood type B* has a substance dissolved in his plasma which will agglutinate erythrocytes containing A. It is called *anti-A*.

We have now described two types of people. One

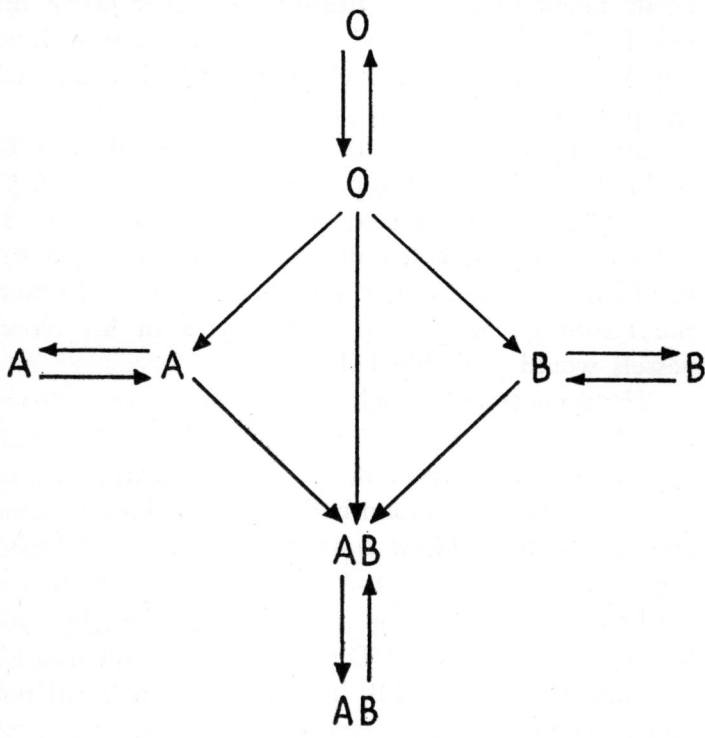

kind has A in his erythrocytes and anti-B in his plasma (the two always go together). The other kind has B in his erythrocytes and anti-A in his plasma.

Suppose, now, a patient who is of blood type A needs blood quickly. A healthy volunteer offers his blood. He is also of blood type A. The donor's blood mingles with the patient's without any bad effect, and the patient's life may be saved.

But suppose the healthy volunteer is of type B. As his blood entered the patient's veins, the anti-B in the patient's plasma would quickly agglutinate the B-containing erythrocytes of the donor. The patient would get no good out of such a transfusion. In fact, the resulting clumped-up erythrocytes in his blood vessels would probably kill him.

The same trouble would result if one were to pump type A blood into a patient whose blood was of type B.

There is a third type of blood. Each erythrocyte of some persons may contain both A and B. Such persons are said to have *blood type AB*. A person of blood type AB has neither anti-A nor anti-B in his plasma. (If he did have anti-A or anti-B, he would agglutinate his own blood and die.) Do you see what this means? Without anti-A or anti-B, he can be given blood not only from a donor of type AB, but also from a donor of type A or B. (Of course, donors of type A and type B have anti-B and anti-A in their plasma, which could agglutinate the patient's AB erythrocytes. This is rarely serious, however. It is the donor's erythrocytes which make trouble. If they are not agglutinated by the patient's plasma, then all is well.)

Blood from a donor of type AB can't be given to a

BLOOD OF VARIOUS TYPES

BLOOD GROUP O

ANTI-A IN PLASMA

ANTI-B IN PLASMA

O-SUBSTANCE IN ERYTHROCYTES

BLOOD GROUP A

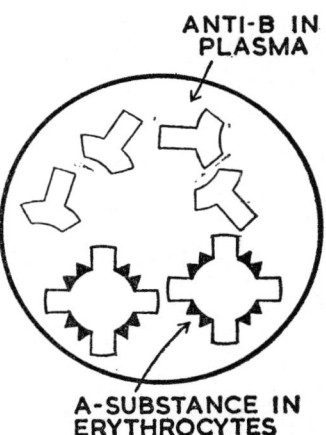

ANTI-B IN PLASMA

A-SUBSTANCE IN ERYTHROCYTES

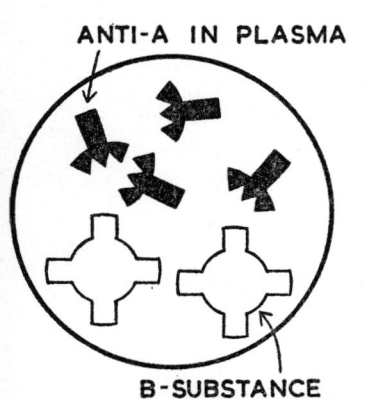

ANTI-A IN PLASMA

B-SUBSTANCE IN ERYTHROCYTES

BLOOD GROUP B

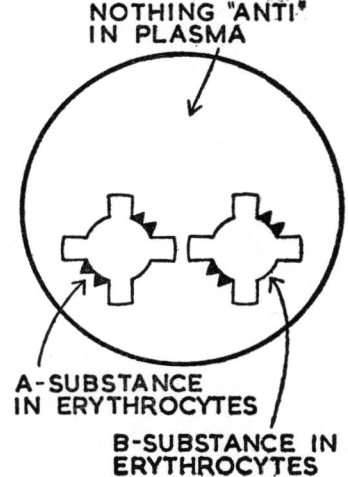

NOTHING "ANTI" IN PLASMA

A-SUBSTANCE IN ERYTHROCYTES

B-SUBSTANCE IN ERYTHROCYTES

patient of type A, for the B in the donor's erythrocytes causes them to be agglutinated by the anti-B in the patient's plasma. The AB donor isn't good for a patient of type B, either, for the A in the donor's erythrocytes causes them to be agglutinated by the anti-A in the patient's plasma.

In other words, an AB donor can give blood only to another AB, but an AB patient can take blood from anyone.

There is still a fourth type of blood. A person may have erythrocytes containing neither A nor B. He is said to be of *blood type O*. Such a person has plasma that contains both anti-A and anti-B. He can't accept blood from anyone but another O. On the other hand, since his erythrocytes contain neither A nor B and so can't make trouble, he can give his blood to a person of any blood type. He is a *universal donor*.

Sometimes it is only necessary to give the patient plasma, and that makes things simpler. Plasma contains A and B, but only in solution; there are no cells to be agglutinated. Furthermore, if the plasma of several donors is mixed, the B in one counteracts the anti-B in another and the A in one counteracts the anti-A in another. It is generally true, then, that plasma can be transferred from any donor to any patient. It is when *whole blood* (plasma plus cells) is needed that the rules of transfusion must be observed.

THE BLOOD GROUPS A, B, AND O

A single gene series controls the production of the blood-group substances we have mentioned. Whether a person is of blood type A, B, AB, or O depends on

AGGLUTINATION

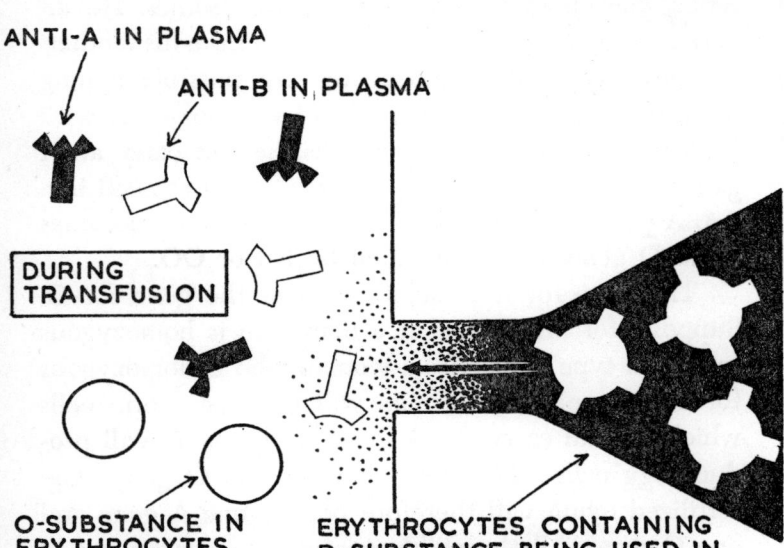

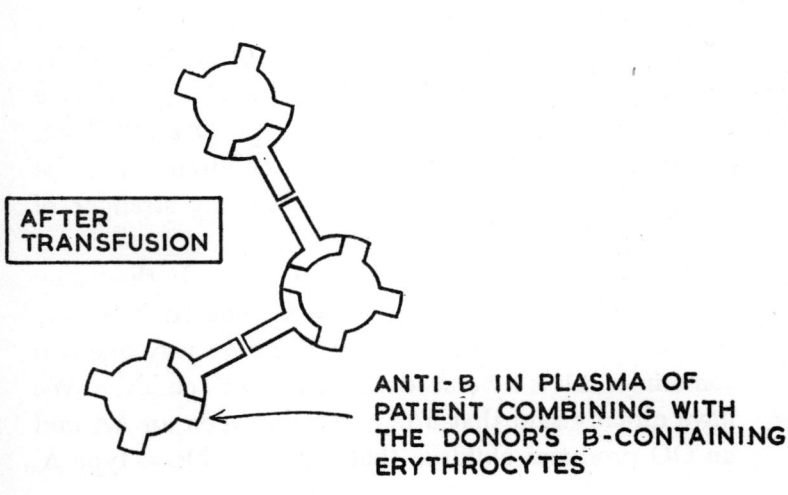

the nature of the genes of that series which he has inherited. Every person has two genes of that gene series, one on each of a pair of chromosomes. He inherits one gene from his father and one from his mother.

Three types of homozygotes are possible among these blood groups. A person can be homozygous with respect to blood group A; that is, he can carry an A gene on both the chromosomes involved. Let's call him AA. A person can have a B gene on both chromosomes or an O gene. He would then be BB or OO.

The gene for A is dominant over the gene for O. Suppose, for instance, that a man who is homozygous for blood type A marries a woman who is homozygous for blood type O. The man will produce sperm cells which will all carry the A gene. The woman will produce egg cells which will all carry the O gene. Any fertilized ovum will therefore possess one A gene and one O gene. All the children of such a marriage will be heterozygous. We can call them AO.

Since A is dominant over O, only the A will appear when scientists test the blood. An AO person will be classified as belonging to blood type A. (Here is a case where a mother is of blood type O and all her children are of blood type A. The children could not give blood to their own mother, but any stranger of blood type O could.)

Suppose a person is of blood type A. Is there any way of telling whether he is homozygous (that is AA) or heterozygous (that is, AO)? The only way one can sometimes tell is by considering the man's children. We have already said that a marriage between an AA and an OO produces children that are all of blood type A.

Suppose, however, that an AO man marries an OO woman. Half of the man's sperm cells contain an A gene and half contain an O gene. All the woman's egg cells contain O genes. You can see that the fertilized eggs could be either AO or OO. In the first case the child would be of blood type A; in the second case he would be of blood type O.

So, you see, if a person of blood type A marries a person of blood type O and has even one child of blood type O, we have found out something. We have discovered that the person of blood type A is AO and not AA. If he were AA, children of blood type O would be impossible.

Of course, as we have just said, an AO-OO marriage can produce either AO or OO fertilized ova. Suppose, just by chance, that all the children produced in the marriage happened to be AO. Here you would have a case where all the children were of blood type A; yet you couldn't be sure that the parent of blood type A was AA. In other words, you can be guided by the type of children produced in a marriage sometimes, but not always.

The gene for blood type B is also dominant over the gene for blood type O. This means that people who are BO are of blood type B. Blood tests cannot tell the difference between BO and BB. The difference shows up (sometimes, not always) in the blood types of the children of such people.

Neither the gene for blood type A nor the gene for blood type B is dominant over the other. Here is a case of incomplete dominance. If an AA person marries a BB person, all the children are AB.

We can now summarize the state of affairs in connection with these blood groups.

1. All people of blood type O are homozygous. They have two O genes. You can see that this must be true. If they had one A gene or one B gene, they would no longer be of bloodtype O.

2. People of blood type A fall into two groups. They can be homozygous, having two A genes, or they can be heterozygous, having one A gene and one O gene. For transfusion the difference doesn't matter. AA blood and AO blood behave exactly alike in transfusion.

3. People of blood type B fall into two groups. They can be homozygous, having two B genes, or they can be heterozygous, having one B gene and one O gene. In transfusion the two groups behave the same.

4. People of blood type AB are all heterozygous. They carry one A gene and one B gene.

SOLOMON'S JUDGMENT

By now you can see one very practical use for blood groups. Suppose some mother had the notion that the hospital had accidentally got her baby mixed up with another baby. She might find out whether this was so by having her blood and the baby's blood tested.

You'll remember, perhaps, that King Solomon, in the Bible, found it necessary once to decide which of two women was the mother of a child. His decision in that matter is the most famous example of the "wisdom of Solomon." With modern blood-group tests the problem might have been very easy.

Suppose, for instance, that one of the women facing Solomon was of blood type O. She would then have

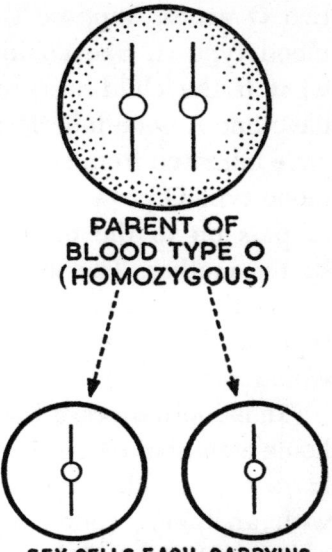

PARENTAGE, POSSIBLE AND IMPOSSIBLE

CASE I

PARENT OF BLOOD TYPE O (HOMOZYGOUS)

SEX CELLS, EACH CARRYING A GENE FOR O

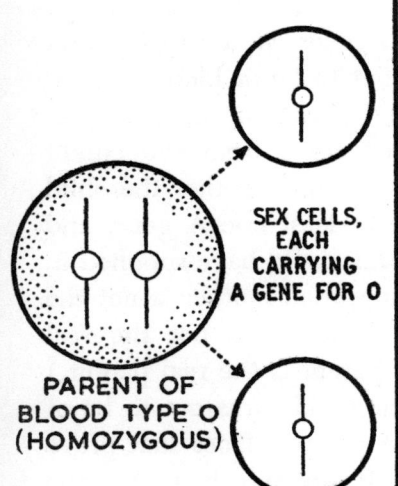

PARENT OF BLOOD TYPE O (HOMOZYGOUS)

SEX CELLS, EACH CARRYING A GENE FOR O

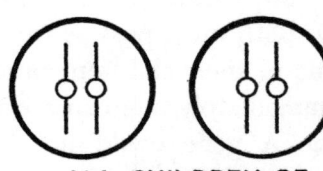

ALL CHILDREN OF BLOOD TYPE O (HOMOZYGOUS)

BLOOD TYPES A, B, AND AB IMPOSSIBLE

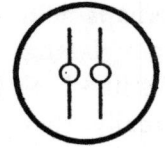 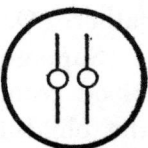

two O genes. Suppose that the other woman was of blood type A. She could be either AA or AO. Now what if the child were of blood type AB? It would have one A gene inherited from one parent and one B gene inherited from the other parent. But the woman of blood type O possesses neither an A gene nor a B gene to pass on to the child, and she could not possibly be the mother. The woman of blood type A could be the mother. (Of course, if both mothers were of blood type A, blood tests involving only this gene series would not help.)

In modern times, a woman of blood type O, bringing home a child of blood type AB from the hospital, would know that the hospital must have mixed up her baby with another's. (Such mix-ups rarely happen.)

Blood tests may also be helpful in deciding whether a certain man is the father of a certain child.

Suppose a man and his wife are both of blood type O. Both must possess two O genes. Now suppose that one of their children turns out to be of blood type A. Immediately one can see that something is wrong, for the A gene could not have come from the child's supposed parents. It doesn't matter whether the child is AA or AO. It must have at least one A gene, and neither its father nor its mother could have supplied it.

In that case either the supposed mother is not the real mother or the supposed father is not the real father. (Or perhaps neither parent is the real parent.)

Suppose, though, that the child turns out to be of blood group O, like both its parents. Does that prove the child is really theirs? It doesn't. It shows the child *might* be theirs, but it doesn't prove it is. The

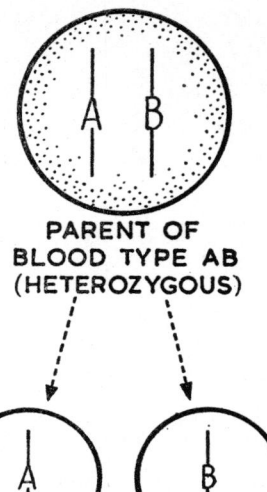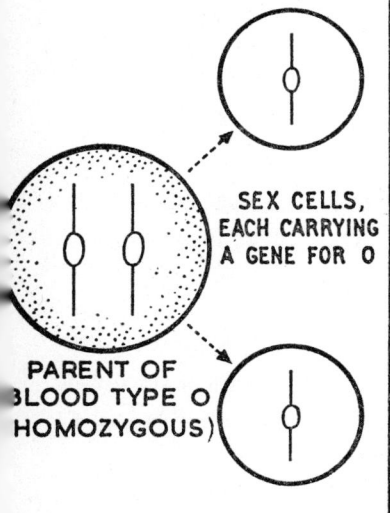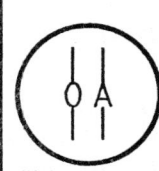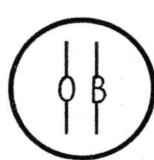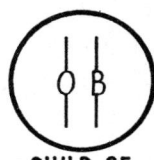

hospital might have mixed it up with another O-type baby. Or the real father might also be of blood group O.

We can make a general rule. A blood test can prove a supposed parent *is not* the real parent. It cannot prove a supposed parent *is* the real parent.

Unless a blood test proves that a supposed parent is not the real parent, it is inconclusive. A decision must then be reached by other types of evidence.

You know enough already to take other cases and see for yourself which blood types are possible among the children of a marriage and which are not. If the father is of blood type O and the mother is of blood type AB, then all the sperm cells carry the O gene, while half of the egg cells carry the A gene and half the B gene. The fertilized ova can only be either AO or BO. It follows that the children of such a marriage must be either of blood type A or of blood type B. Children of blood type O or blood type AB are impossible. This is an interesting case because it is one in which it is impossible for children to be exactly like either their mother or their father in this physical characteristic.

Here is another interesting case. Suppose the father is of blood type A and the mother of blood type B. The father might be AA or AO; it would be impossible to tell which. The mother might be BB or BO; again impossible to tell which. Suppose they were AO and BO. In that case half of the sperm cells would carry the A gene and half the O gene. Half of the egg cells would carry the B gene and half the O gene. The fertilized ova could possess any of these combinations of genes:

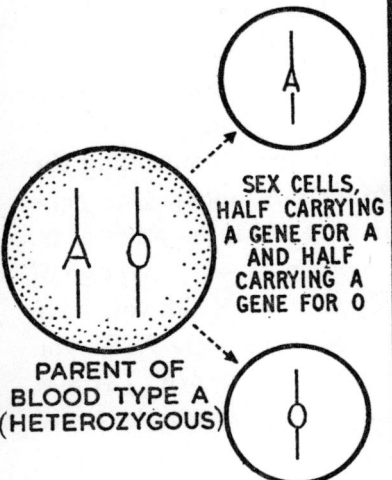

OO (blood type O), AO (blood type A), BO (blood type B), and AB (blood type AB).

So you see that, if one parent is of blood type A and the other of blood type B, the children could belong to any of the four types. It would be impossible to prove that any child at all did not belong to this couple if only this gene series were considered.

OTHER BLOOD GROUPS

It is not necessary to give up in despair over this A—B marriage we have just discussed. The scientist who tests blood is not at the end of his rope. There are two varieties of A, called A_1 and A_2, and these can be told apart by careful testing. This may help in making the decision. (As far as transfusions are concerned, it doesn't matter which variety is present in either donor or patient.)

Then, too, there are other blood-group substances in the erythrocytes which are controlled by different gene series altogether. They are inherited completely independently of the A, B, and O genes.

There is, for instance, a gene series controlling the so-called M and N blood-group substances. One gene of that series causes the formation of M, the other of N. Neither is dominant over the other. If you have two of the M genes, you are of *blood type M*. If you have two of the N genes, you are of *blood type N*. If you have one of each, you are of *blood type MN*. (The M and N blood groups are of no importance in transfusion, by the way.)

Now the M and N blood groups have no connection with the A, B, and O blood groups. A person can be of blood type M, N, or MN, regardless of whether he is also of blood type A, B, O, or AB.

Suppose, then, that both parents are of blood type O and so are all their children. Only O genes are involved. But suppose that both parents are also of blood type M and so are all their children except one. That one is of blood type MN. He must have got the N gene somewhere. One or both of the supposed parents can't be the real one.

Still another gene series controls the formation of a number of blood-group substances of the *Rh series*. (The "Rh" refers to the fact that they were first discovered in experiments with the Rhesus monkey.) There are a large number of genes in this series, and as many as a dozen different Rh types (including some heterozygous ones) can be tested for. These, too, can be used to help decide parentage problems. The more types of blood groups we use, the greater the chance of settling such questions satisfactorily.

There are difficulties, too, of course. The methods used to test for the different blood groups can be quite complicated, especially in the case of Rh. It is necessary to understand the exact way in which all the various Rh genes can be inherited. It is also necessary to be certain that you have the proper chemicals to work with. (The most important chemicals are in the liquid portion of clotted blood, called *serum*, obtained from certain people or animals. It is sometimes a very delicate matter to determine whether the serum being used is just right for the purpose.) To run blood tests properly, an experienced laboratory man is required, and there are not very many of those.

Blood tests, by the way, can also be used in murder cases. It is possible to tell whether a blood stain is human or not. If it is human blood, one can sometimes tell whether it is of the same blood type as that of the murdered man. Even ancient Egyptian mummies have been successfully tested for blood type.

9

Races at Last

THE ADVANTAGES OF BLOOD GROUPS

A PERSON'S BLOOD GROUP is one of his physical characteristics, just as a dark skin may be, or blue eyes or a hooked nose. Like other physical characteristics, blood groups can be used to divide mankind into races.

You may ask at once: But would they be any better for the purpose than skin color or any of the other physical characteristics we have talked about in this book?

The answer is that in some ways they would be.

1. They are "hidden" characteristics. You can't tell a man's blood group by looking at him. This reserves race classification to scientists who are interested in the development and evolution of man. It keeps a person from making judgments of his own about his neighbor's race and from building up superstitions and prejudices about it.

2. Unlike the more familiar physical characteristics, blood groups are inherited in known ways. The A, B, and O blood groups are controlled by a single gene series consisting of three genes. The M and N blood groups are controlled by a single gene series

consisting of two genes. The Rh blood groups are controlled by a single gene series consisting of eight genes. In each case, we know which genes are dominant over which.

3. A man's blood group is determined the instant the fertilized ovum is formed and remains the same till the day he dies. Even after death tissues can be tested for blood groups. Blood groups aren't affected by age or diet or exposure to sunlight or by any kind of chemical or medical treatment. None of the things that affect the physical characteristics usually used to determine race will affect blood groups. Blood groups are permanent.

4. With one exception, which we will mention later in this chapter, blood groups have no drastic effect on the health of a man, the length of his life, when or whom he marries, or the number or health of his children. That means that the blood-group genes are all passed on from generation to generation according to pure chance. Blood groups would therefore show how human beings have mixed with one another, for there would be no confusion due to the workings of natural selection. (We talked about natural selection on page 122.)

THE KEY WORD: FREQUENCY

The simplest situation we could imagine would be to have all people who live in one part of the world belong to blood type O; all people in another part of the world belong to blood type A, and so on. Actually, of course, nothing like this happens at all. The various blood groups are found all over the world.

THE KEY WORD: FREQUENCY 147

However, they are not found in the same proportions everywhere.

There are some tribes of American Indians in which as many as 98 percent of the people tested are of blood group O. The rest are of blood group A. Other Indian tribes have a great many people of blood group A, some as many as 80 percent of the people. The rest are of blood group O. Few, if any, "pure-blooded" American Indians, however, are of blood type B or AB.

Inhabitants of Asia are more commonly of blood type B than are people who live elsewhere. A group of people in Bengal, India, were tested, and it was found that 40 percent of them were of blood type B. Only 32 percent were of blood type O, and only 20 percent of blood type A. The rest were of blood type AB.

In general, over all the world, blood type O is the most common. Blood type A is next, and blood type B is after that. Blood type AB is the least common. It is very rare for even as many as 10 percent of a population to be of blood type AB.

Scientists try to go further than just the blood types. They try to determine how many of each type of gene are present. For instance, we know that every person of blood group O has two O genes and every person of blood group AB has one A gene and one B gene. However, a person of blood type A may have an O gene or may not. The same is true of a person of blood type B.

Fortunately, there are ways of calculating from blood-group figures how many O genes are hidden in persons of blood groups A and B. (You can't tell which particular persons have them, of course.) Once you've calculated the number of hidden O genes, you can tell exactly what percentage of each gene is present in a particular population.

In this way one determines the *gene frequencies* in a gene series.

Let's see what we get out of calculating our gene frequencies. Tests on the population of London show that, of the A-B-O gene series, 70 percent are O genes, 25 percent are A genes, and 5 percent are B genes.

In the city of Kharkov, Russia, on the other hand, tests show that of that gene series, 60 percent are O genes, 25 percent are A genes, and 15 percent are B genes.

Suppose that a sample of blood is brought to a scientist and he is told: "This blood is taken from either a Londoner or a Kharkovite. Can you tell me which?" The answer is, "No!" All three types of genes are found in both cities. But suppose a thousand samples of blood are brought, and they come either from a thousand Londoners or from a thousand Kharkovites. Now the scientist has a very good chance of making the right choice, for the gene frequency of B is three times as high in Kharkov as in London. If he gets a small number of blood group B and AB in his samples, they're from London. If he gets a fairly large number, they're from Kharkov.

In fact, if we pick convenient gene series such as that for the blood-group substances, we can have a genetic definition of race as follows: A race is a group of people with a gene frequency different from those of other groups of people.

MAPPING THE WORLD BY GENES

Gene frequencies for the A-B-O series have been determined for many parts of the world. Using these figures, it is possible to draw a special kind of world map.

Suppose that you take an outline map of the world and decide to place a dot wherever there is some population group in which the B gene occurs in 10 people out of a hundred. When this done, you can draw a line through all the dots you have made. Such a line would be an *isogene*. It is a line along which the populations have similar frequencies as far as the B gene is concerned.

You can also make dots wherever the B gene frequency is 15 out of a hundred, 20 out of a hundred, 25 out of a hundred. In each case, you can draw a new isogene.

When you are done, your outline map is crossed by curving lines, and you can mark different portions of the map accordingly as in the map on page 150. In Spain, the B gene frequency is less than 5 out of a hundred. If you study the map, though, you see that if you start in Spain and travel eastward across Europe, the B gene frequency increases steadily. By the time you reach France, it is over 5 out of a hundred. By the time you reach Germany, it is 10 out of a hundred. In western Russia it is 15 out of a hundred. At the boundary of Asia it is 20 out of a

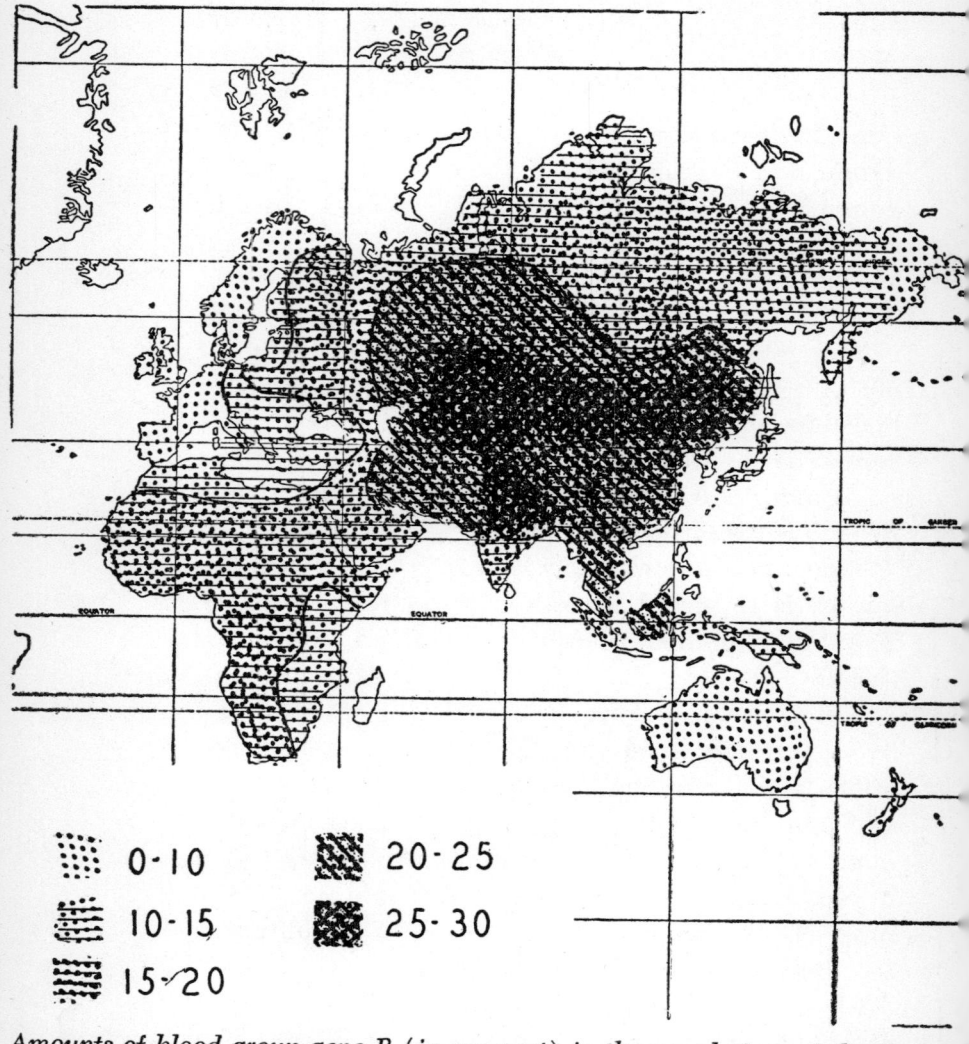

Amounts of blood group gene B (in per cent) in the populations of the Eastern hemisphere.

hundred and shortly thereafter 25 out of a hundred.

The gene frequencies for B are highest in the area surrounded by the isogene for 25 out of a hundred. This area includes central Asia, Manchuria, Iran, and northern India. As you move away from this region in any direction, the gene frequency of blood group B falls off. The areas that are farthest from this region are lowest in B.

(The very low frequency of B in Australia and the Americas applies only to the native population, the Indians and the Aborigines. The Europeans who have emigrated to the Americas and to Australia have the same gene frequencies as their ancestors since they brought the B gene with them.)

When a small area of the world is very carefully and thoroughly studied, a detailed isogene map can be made for it. Such a study has been made in Japan, for instance, and it has been found that the A gene has its highest frequency in an area near the western tip of the country. The frequency is over 30 out of a hundred there. As one travels eastward across Japan, the frequency gradually declines until at the eastern tip it is less than 24 out of a hundred.

HUMAN HISTORY BY GENES

Now we are ready to see how genetics can help us understand human history.

In the first place, we must understand that the O, A, and B genes are all very old. They are not the result of recent mutations. For one thing, tests on Egyptian mummies show the three blood-group genes to be present there in about the same proportions as in modern Egyptians.

Furthermore, blood-group substances O, A, and B, or substances very like them, are found in gorillas, orangutans, and other apes, as well as in monkeys and lower animals. In fact, when blood technicians want a supply of A substance, they get it out of ground-up hog stomach. Out of ground-up horse stomach they can get something very much like B substance.

It certainly seems, then, that the O, A, and B genes are the general property of many animals, just as the gene for forming melanin is. Mankind has had all three from the very earliest times.

But then, you may wonder, why is it that the Aborigines and American Indians have practically no B gene, and that some Indian tribes have practically no A gene either?

This is no easy matter to solve, and no one has proposed a theory which satisfies everyone.

About the most reasonable theory, so far, is one which supposes that modern man first developed in central Asia at a time when its climate was more favorable than it is now. This earliest group of modern man may have had gene frequencies of 25 A, 15 B, and 60 O out of every hundred A-B-O blood-group genes.

This is about the gene frequency found in central Asia today.

As the population increased, small groups would spread out, looking for new hunting grounds. These small groups would settle down in the new territory and could become the ancestors of large populations eventually.

Now remember that the predictions of probability hold best for large numbers. (We've mentioned this before.) When we say that out of every 100 blood-group genes there are 25 A genes, what we really mean is that if a large number of cases are taken, that's how the results will average out.

Suppose you test 500 people, for instance. Each person has two genes of the A-B-O gene series; that makes 1,000 genes altogether. Suppose you find a total of 253 A genes. That's pretty close, since you expect 250 A genes. It's 3 off, but what's 3 in a thousand? Not much.

Suppose you take 50 people, with 100 genes, and find 28 genes for A instead of 25. That's still only 3 off, but 3 in a hundred amounts to more than 3 in a thousand.

Finally, suppose you take 2 persons with 4 blood-group genes. You might easily find 4 genes for A. You expect only 1; so you're still only 3 off. But now 3 out of 4 is very important indeed. In fact, it would mean that these 2 persons have only genes for A, no genes for B and O at all.

Therefore, when a small group breaks off from a parent population and goes off to a new territory, it may happen that there is no B gene, let us say, among them. Or there may be a few B genes present, and the owners may happen to die or be killed before they have any children. In either case, you now have a group with only A and O genes. If this group is allowed to remain in isolation, and if no new emigrants from central Asia join them, all their descendants will have only A and O genes.

This is what may actually have happened. From central Asia, separate groups may have reached western Europe, northern Africa, eastern and southern Asia, Australia. None of them would have had any genes for B. Their gene frequencies would have been, say, 30 A and 70 O out of every hundred.

You may ask, "Isn't that too much of a coincidence? Why should it always be the B gene that disappears?" Well, the B gene is the least common to begin with, only 15 out of a hundred. Therefore, in any small group, it is the one which is most likely to disappear.

To go back to our migrating people, imagine now the new inhabitants of northeastern Asia, with only the A gene and O gene among them. They multiply also, and again small groups break away. One such crosses the Bering Strait into Alaska. In this small group, the A gene (which is less than half as common as the O gene among them) either did not exist or happened to die out.

Slowly, the immigrants and their descendants spread throughout the Americas, giving rise to Indian tribes which are almost pure O. Later, other groups, carrying A this time, may have entered Alaska. By modern times, the new groups had only the chance to drift down through North America. For that reason, South American Indians would remain almost entirely O while North American Indians would in some cases have considerable quantities of the A gene.

After that, as we approach closer to historical times and as the human population on Earth increases, there were larger and larger emigrations out of central Asia. These were large enough to carry the B gene with them. The regions that were nearest central Asia, such as Manchuria and northern India, got the most. Eastern Europe got the most in that continent, and the B gene trickles off as you move westward. Northeastern Africa got the most in that continent, and the B gene trickles off as you move westward and southward.

Apparently the first waves of B just reached the northern tip of Australia in quite recent times, and it is only now beginning to drift southward among the Aboriginal population. The American Indians were never reached by peoples carrying the B gene, however, until first the Eskimos arrived and later Europeans began migrating into the Americas after the discoveries of Columbus.

THE HUMAN RACES, BY GENES

Suppose, then, that groups of human beings, splitting off from the original central Asian population, had different gene frequencies as far as the A, B, and O blood groups were concerned. It is very likely that the gene frequencies with respect to other physical characteristics were also changed. If these groups multiplied in isolation, they would finally become populations with marked differences in appearance. (This state of affairs is known as *genetic drift*.) Let us see whether we can detect these different-appearing groups or races, by just considering the A, B, and O blood groups, the M and N, and the Rh blood groups.

The American Indians and the Australian Aborigines are alike in possessing A and O and little or no B. They differ, however, in the M and N genes. Throughout most of the world the frequencies are about 55 M and 45 N out of every hundred. The exceptions are among the American Indians and the Australian Aborigines. The Indians are low in N and high in M; the Aborigines, on the other hand, are low in M and high in N.

The people of Asia and those of Africa generally have higher frequencies of the B gene than other people do. They differ from each other in the Rh series. The Asian peoples have a high frequency of a gene called Rh^z to distinguish it from the other genes of the Rh series. The African peoples, on the other hand, have a high frequency of another Rh gene called Rh^o.

The most troublesome peoples to pin down are those that live in Europe. Here a problem arises in the Rh blood-group series.

In order to explain the problem, let's just say a few words about the Rh series. One of the Rh genes is usually written as rh (with a small "r"). The rh gene is recessive to all the other genes in the Rh series. Therefore, it is only when a person is homozygous for rh (that is, has two rh genes) that it can be detected. Such a person is said to be *Rh-negative*. A person with only one rh gene or none at all is *Rh-positive*.

Rh-negative blood is one type which can have a drastic effect on human health. (Remember, we said at the beginning of the chapter that there was one.) Sometimes a mother is Rh-negative and her unborn baby is Rh-positive (having inherited one of the other Rh genes from the father). When this happens, some of the baby's erythrocytes may be destroyed and other serious damage also results. Consequently, the baby will die before birth or very shortly after.

Nowadays, modern medicine can handle these babies, once they are born, by means of transfusions. In earlier times, however, no help was possible. As a result, you would expect the rh gene to disappear slowly. Rh-negative mothers would have fewer living children, and so the rh gene would be passed on less frequently than the other genes in the series.

Sure enough, the American, Australian, and Asiatic groups have little or no rh gene. The African group contains a small quantity of rh gene. The inhabitants of Europe (including Americans and Australians who are descended from Europeans), however, have a good deal of the rh gene; about one out of seven among them is Rh-negative.

Why should this be?

One answer is that there may once have been in Europe a race that was entirely or almost entirely Rh-negative. (That would be safe enough, you see. If everyone were Rh-negative, there would be no problem. It is only when both Rh-positive and Rh-negative are present that the trouble starts.) If there was such an Rh-negative race, then an Rh-positive group may have entered Europe later and intermixed with the earlier group. The one out of seven Rh-negatives in modern Europeans and their descendants would be the result. There may not yet have been time for the rh gene to disappear since the mixture took place. (And some of the rh genes may have drifted far enough south to show up among the Africans.)

Such an early European race seems to have turned up in the group of people called Basques. These people live in the Pyrenees Mountains (which form the boundary between France and Spain) and adjacent regions. The Basques have interested anthropologists because their language is like no other language in the world. Now it turns out that their blood groups are like no others either. One out of three Basques is Rh-negative. This means that the rh gene frequency among them is 60 out of a hundred. The Basques, then, are thought to be descendants of the early race; they hadn't mixed much with the later invaders because they lived in remote mountain fastnesses.

Now we can summarize our six genetic races:*

1. *Australian* (Aboriginal): low B or none, low M, no A_2
2. *American* (Indian): low B or none, low N, no A_2
3. *Asian:* High B, high Rh^z, no A_2
4. *African:* High B, high Rh^o, some rh, high A_2
5. *European:* moderately high rh, moderate B, moderate A_2
6. *Early European:* very high rh, no B

The accompanying map shows the way the six races (plus a seventh race which is less clear-cut) divide the world. The blank areas in northern Africa, in west-

* The genes for O and A are so widespread among all groups of people that they are nearly useless in racial classification.

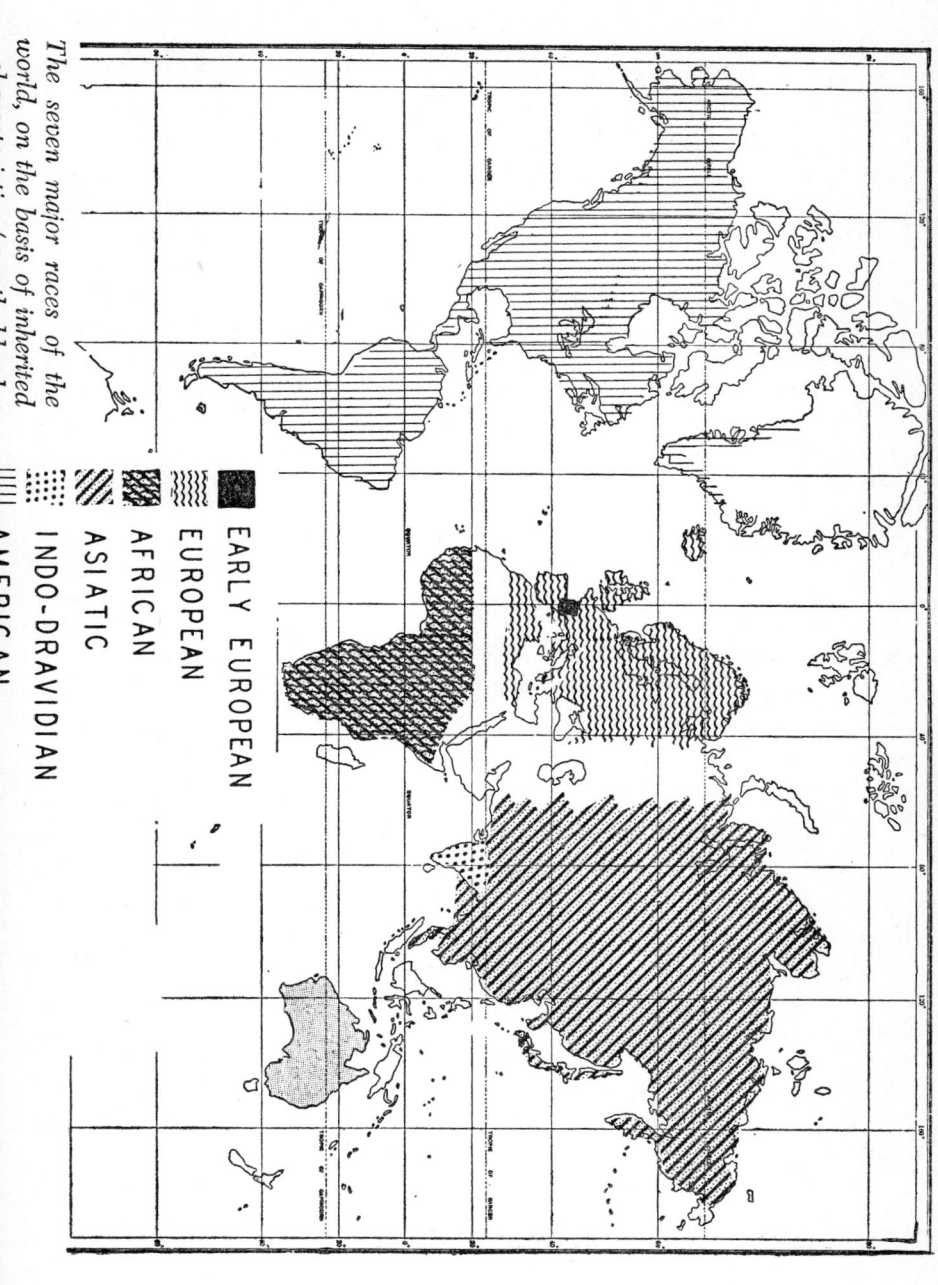

The seven major races of the world, on the basis of inherited characteristics (mostly blood...

- EARLY EUROPEAN
- EUROPEAN
- AFRICAN
- ASIATIC
- INDO-DRAVIDIAN
- AMERICAN

ern Asia, and along the East Indies are regions where blood-group studies have not yet been carried on in sufficient detail. (The map does not take account of the emigration of Europeans since 1700. If it did, North America and Australia would have to be marked mostly for the European race, and so would the edges of South America.)

It is very important to remember that members of a particular race do *not* all have the same blood-group genes. The Asian and African races, for instance, have high frequencies of B, compared with other races, yet individual Asians and Africans may not have the B gene. In fact, the majority of them don't. This method of determining race by genes works only on groups, then, and not on single individuals!

It may seem that we've ended up, after all this, with only a new way of looking at the same old races.

But actually we can go further. Already, in the new system, we have separated the Aboriginal from the Negro; both, by the old system, were members of the "Black Race." The "black" Dravidians of India are not closely related to either the "black" Aborigines or the "black" Negroes. We have made a distinction between Basques (who are certainly members of the "White Race") and other Europeans.

Furthermore, it is possible to divide the American Indians into two groups, depending on whether they are high or low in A gene frequency. The inhabitants of India and Pakistan seem to be different in some respects from their neighbors and may form the seventh race we referred to above. This might be classified as an "Indo-Dravidian race," intermediate between the

European and the Asian, but closer to the European. We can follow immigration waves which we could not follow if we used skin color or some other obvious physical characteristic. For instance, a group of immigrants high in A must have entered western Japan from Korea in the not distant past and spread eastward. That would account for the variation of frequency in the A gene in different parts of Japan.

As we learn more about the blood-group genes, and about other genes, too, and as we test more and more people all over the earth, we can expect to be able to trace man's evolution more exactly and to learn the stages by which he has populated the world.

10

The Present and Future of Race

WHAT ABOUT RACISM?

IN CHAPTER NINE we listed six races differing from one another in blood-group gene frequencies. There are also differences in other gene frequencies among these races. We feel sure of that. The question now is: What can genes tell us about race superiority or inferiority? Are members of any one race born superior to members of any other? Is there any value in the theories of racism?

The first thing to remember is that the word "superior" is not easy to define or to get clear in your mind. Superior in what way or under what conditions?

A dark skin might be better suited to a tropical climate. A light skin might be better suited to a northern climate. Both types of skin might do quite well in an in-between climate.

The answer to the question whether a "race" is superior or not could depend on the particular characteristic and the environment you were thinking of.

But you may wonder: What about intelligence? That is the important thing that separates man from the lower animals. Is one human race superior to another in brain power from birth? Can it progress faster, develop science faster, build bigger and better cities and civilizations, all because it happens to have genes that develop a superior type of mind?

We cannot say. We do not know how genes control intelligence or how many genes are involved. We do not know very much about the chemistry of the brain. We do not know very much about how intelligence is inherited.

There is every reason to think, though, that intelligence is controlled by a rather complicated set-up of genes. It must also be strongly influenced by environment.

It seems to be true, that highly intelligent parents have intelligent children more often than do parents of normal or less than normal intelligence. Talents such as musical ability frequently seem to run in families. Yet how much is due to inherited genes and how much to environment?

Children born to intelligent parents are brought up by intelligent people who stimulate their minds. They are surrounded by books from an early age. Their curiosity is encouraged. They have the opportunity for education.

In the same way, people born of musical parents are surrounded by a musical kind of environment. They listen to music frequently and hear music discussed. They grow accustomed to musical instruments. They are encouraged to learn music.

To repeat, then, if children resemble their parents in such things as intelligence and musical ability, how much of the resemblance is due to genes and how much to their surroundings? We cannot say.

Our ignorance concerning how genes control intelligence is shown whenever a child of great talent is born of ordinary parents, as sometimes happens—or whenever extraordinary parents have quite ordinary children, as often happens. There is no way geneticists can predict either happening, or explain it.

Certainly, though, it can be said that, whatever the gene or genes that control intelligence and the various kinds of talent, no one race has a monopoly, or even a lion's share, of them. People with all sorts of mental characteristics (both good and bad) and with all sorts of talents are produced by all races.

The problem of intelligence is especially complicated because we do not have a fool-proof method of measuring or judging intelligence.

The method generally used is to make up a series of questions for children to answer in order to see how well and quickly they think. These are called *intelligence tests*. If a thousand five-year-olds take such a test, their average mark, you decide, is what a five-year-old ought to get on that particular test. The average mark of a thousand ten-year-olds is what you will expect of a ten-year-old. You can do the same for other ages.

Suppose, now, that a particular five-year-old actually gets just the average mark for his age class. That means he has a "mental age" of five as well as a physical age of five. He is said to have an *intelligence quotient* of 100.

The intelligence quotient is determined by dividing the mental age by the physical age and then multiplying the answer by 100. If another five-year-old got a mark which was equal to the average mark of the ten-year-olds, he would have a "mental age" of 10. His intelligence quotient would be 10 divided by 5, multiplied by 100. The answer is 200. On the other hand, a boy of 10 who got a mark equal to the average for five-year-olds would have an intelligence quotient of 50. "Intelligence quotient" is usually abbreviated as I.Q.

Naturally, this sort of testing is not accurate. We can't say that a person with an I.Q. of 101 is more intelligent than one with an I.Q. of 99. The tests aren't that finely worked out. Instead, I.Q. ranges are established. Thus it is usual to consider people normal in intelligence if their I.Q. is somewhere near 100—that is, somewhere in the range from 70 to 130. People with an I.Q. of less than 70 are considered inferior in intelligence. People with an I.Q. higher than 130 are considered superior in intelligence.

This sounds good as far as it goes, but the trouble lies in the tests themselves. How can we be certain that the questions they include are a fair measure of intelligence? Suppose a group of people took two different tests made up by two different groups of scientists. Would everyone get the same I.Q. rating on both tests? Probably not. It could very well be that John is brighter than Bob according to one test, while Bob is brighter than John according to the other test.

Why should this be so?

Your ability to answer a certain question depends not only on your intelligence, you see, but also on your surroundings and on the things you are accustomed to. A five-year-old child brought up in the city might not be able to answer questions about cows. He might not be able to say how many legs a cow has or at which end you get the milk. A five-year-old child brought up on a farm might not be able to say whether it's a high building or a low one that needs an elevator. He might not know that an elevator moves up and down, not backward and forward. Each child would do quite well on questions that would stump the other. For that reason the two children might do quite differently on different tests even though they were really of equal intelligence.

That is one of the reasons why one cannot simply give a test to a group of Australian Aborigines and to a group of Americans and expect to be able to say that one race is more intelligent than the other. Americans would probably do much better in the usual intelligence tests, which are made up by Americans. On the other hand, an Australian Aboriginal might make up an intelligence test with all sorts of simple questions on boomerangs, animal-tracking, kangaroos, and stone knives. Then the Aborigines would do very well, and the Americans would almost surely get marks indicating inferior intelligence.

Some people might say: Why bother to measure intelligence? Isn't the world situation all the evidence that is needed? See how the European peoples and their descendants have built an advanced civilization while other races have remained primitive. Isn't that proof enough that the European race is superior to the rest?

That is not really evidence enough.

To be sure, the Europeans were the first to develop

an industrial civilization, and in the last two hundred years they have therefore managed to outshine other peoples in some ways. Still, it took them thousands of years to get to that point. Furthermore, the other races are adopting the industrial and scientific civilization without difficulty.

During most of the last six thousand years, in fact, Asia and Africa were ahead of Europe. Advanced civilizations developed in Egypt, the Near East, India, and China while the European peoples were practicing human sacrifice and painting themselves blue. It could well be that, in the future, groups other than the Europeans will again take the lead. We can't draw any conclusions merely from what happens to be the situation at this moment. It just isn't safe.

And even if some day we were to decide that such and such a group of people were superior in intelligence, on the average, to another group, it would still be only an average. A particular individual of the "inferior" group might still be more intelligent than a particular individual of the "superior" group.

From all we know of genetics today, then, we can say that anyone who believes in "race superiority" is ignorant or misled. There is still no scientific evidence for the superiority or inferiority of any race.

You may be telling yourself at this point: There doesn't seem to be much use to this notion of race if it tells us so little.

And that is exactly what we must realize. The whole notion of race is really quite useless to the average man. Except for certain unscientific and superstitious ideas, it tells him nothing. The notion of race is useful only to anthropologists and other scientists for tracing human migrations and so forth. The rest of us might just as well stop worrying about the whole thing.

We should consider all human beings as individuals to be judged for themselves alone, and not as members of any race. This is not only the kindest way to behave, but also, as this book has tried to show, the most scientific way as well.

WHAT ABOUT THE FUTURE?

Now that scientists have learned something about genes and about how characteristics are inherited, can they say what will happen to man in the future? How will he evolve? Will he grow more intelligent? Will he become extinct?

If we were speaking of any other species, there would be no great problem. We would know that the species would have to continue to develop in such a way as to fit its environment or perish. As its environment changed, it would change. If its environment changed too quickly, or if the species didn't happen to hit on enough of the right mutations, the species would decline in numbers or even become extinct.

All this is true of the human species, too, but man's case is a little more complicated. Unlike other creatures, man can, to some extent, control his own environment. Other creatures must develop thick fur or warm feathers or layers of fat if they are to live in the polar regions. Man need only use the furs of other animals and build the right kind of houses. In that way he can keep his almost hairless skin and be none the worse for it.

This sounds as though controlling your environment were a good thing, and so it is sometimes. It might also be a bad thing. Let us see how.

In the first place there is the question of war. Battle among members of the same species is one way of making sure that the stronger survive. In the days when men fought one another with teeth and muscles, or even with hand weapons like knives and clubs, the stronger and more skillful men ordinarily won. (Of course, a longer knife or a larger club helped a bit, too.) On the whole, war in those days could act as a means of natural selection for some types of physical characteristics, such as greater strength, increased nimbleness, and sharper sight.

Once long-distance weapons were invented, first the arrow and eventually bullets and bombs, it became the better weapon that counted more and more. An invalid behind a machine gun, for instance, might kill a hundred athletes armed with rifles. Many times in recent history, in fact, war has kept the weak alive at the expense of the strong. Soldiers, you see, are chosen from among the most physically fit of the population. The weak and handicapped remain behind and are often safe for that reason. The strong and healthy go into battle, and many are killed.

Modern science also reverses the effects of natural selection by preserving undesirable genes. In a primitive society, for example, good eyesight is important. A man with good eyesight can see danger sooner. If he is hunting for food, he can see a deer at a greater distance. He can aim his spear or arrow at it better. A man with poor eyesight would not live as well or as long as one with good eyesight. For this reason, man has developed more efficient eyes through the ages. The poor genes were not transmitted to the next generation as frequently as the good ones; and, if new genes developed by mutation, they did not last long.

Nowadays, though, it is easy to correct many eye defects simply by wearing the proper eyeglasses. Many people wear glasses all their lives and find their poor eyesight no handicap at all. They live just as long and as well as people with naturally excellent eyes. In this way, genes that result in poor eyesight are preserved from generation to generation. New mutations for poor eyesight are added to those genes, and eyes grow poorer rather than better.

More serious conditions are also preserved by modern science. There is a disease called diabetes, which involves the chemistry of the body. People with diabetes cannot turn their food into energy in the proper manner. Until the early part of the twentieth century, diabetes could not be treated properly. People with diabetes lost weight, were increasingly ill, and did not live long. Now, however, doctors make use of a chemical called insulin, which enables people with diabetes to live normal lives. This was a great advance of medical knowledge, and the men who discovered insulin received the Nobel Prize. Just the same, it does allow the genes for diabetes to be passed on more and more from generation to generation.

A third way in which modern man interferes with the process of evolution has just arisen in the twentieth century. We have mentioned it already. Beginning with X-rays and continuing now with atom bombs and hydrogen bombs, mankind has been producing types of radiation which are known to affect genes. They are known to increase the number of mutations. Since most mutations are for the worse, the danger may be a very terrible one. In other species, increasing the number of mutations may merely mean an increased number of deaths among the mutated individuals. It would still be the strong and healthy that survived. Man, however, would try to save the weakened members of his own species and would often succeed, too.

THE IMPROVEMENT OF MAN

All this makes it look as though the human race were headed for destruction. We hope not, certainly. But is there any way of preventing destruction? One thing that would help, of course, is for mankind to avoid war, particularly atomic war. Another is to take special precautions in the use of atomic power, even in peacetime.

What about the bad results of the preservation of the weak and handicapped? Is there anything that can be done about that?

Few people would be so cruel as to suggest that people who are handicapped in some way be killed or allowed to die. There are some, though, who think that the only way to solve the problem is to prevent the "unfit" from having children. In this way the undesirable genes would not be passed on. This sort of program is called *eugenics*.

It might seem to you that this is very reasonable. After all, by controlling mating among domestic animals, we have "improved the breed." Modern cows give more milk and better beef than the cows of ancient times. We have developed sheep that give more wool, hens that lay more eggs, faster and stronger horses, intelligent and faithful dogs, and so on. Couldn't man's "breed" be improved in the same way?

It is not as easy as all that. It is all very well to breed an animal with only one thing in mind: milk, wool, eggs, or something like that. The human being, however, has numerous good qualities, and we want to save them all. Some of the most desirable good qualities, such as great genius in science or literature, or great nobility of mind, are so far beyond our understanding that we wouldn't even know how to begin breeding for them.

Let us take a simple example. We have talked about the use of glasses as an example of taking care of the unfit. Would the human race benefit if we refused to let near-sighted people have children? We might produce a race of sharp-eyed people, which is a good thing in a way. But think of all the good qualities near-sighted people might have: intelligence, physical strength, immunity to diseases, and so on. (Naturally, not all near-sighted people would have all these good qualities, but some might.) Are we ready to throw away all these good genes in order to get rid of one bad gene, the results of which, after all, can be corrected easily enough these days?

Furthermore, even if you stop the "unfit" from having children, you will not get rid of an undesirable gene very quickly. Suppose, for instance, you decide that the only way to get rid of diabetes is absolutely to prevent people with diabetes from having children. Well, since diabetes, like most undesirable characteristics, is probably controlled by a recessive gene, many people may carry the gene for diabetes and never show the disease. Diabetes would keep showing up in future generations. In the long run it would die out, of course (except that it would crop up periodically as the result of mutation), but it would take a long time. To reduce diabetes by 99 percent would take over 2,000 years.

So, you see, a eugenics program is not as simple as it might seem. Even by taking the most severe measures, we could only remove undesirable genes very slowly. In doing that, we would create a great deal of unhappiness and tragedy, and we wouldn't even be sure that we were making it possible for future generations to be healthier and happier. We might be getting rid of desirable genes at the same time.

Before we can be certain of improving humanity by deciding who ought to have children and who ought not, it is necessary for us to learn a great deal more about genetics. That is the important thing, knowledge and more knowledge. Genetics, especially human genetics, is still a terribly young science, and much remains to be learned.

Meanwhile, while we are waiting to learn enough about genetics to do ourselves some good, the ordinary course of events may help us out.

People are moving about the world more than ever before. With the invention of the steamboat and the locomotive, the automobile and finally the airplane, it has become easier and easier for people to travel from one part of the Earth to another. Parts of the world which have been quite isolated in the past are isolated no longer. In recent years, moreover, armies have marched over many parts of the world. Even today American troops are still stationed in remote regions.

What this amounts to is that there are more and more opportunities for mixture among people of different groups. This means that there may be an opportunity for new combinations of genes in the children.

This would have several effects. First, it would make the different races on Earth less distinct. Each race developed in the first place because the isolation of small groups allowed genetic drift and selection to act. Then, living in isolation, the descendants of these small groups kept their mutations to themselves.

Now the mutated genes that mark off one race from another would get an opportunity to appear in combination with one another.

Such new types of gene combinations would result in greater variations among mankind. There would be more people who combined undesirable qualities, but there would also be more people who combined desirable qualities. There would be more subnormal people, perhaps, but there would be also more people of unusual talent. Since the important advances of mankind are probably due to the few individuals of unusual ability produced each generation, producing more of them would be very good. Some of these individuals might help advance genetics to the point where we needed to wait for chance no longer.

The United States is itself a land with a population in which new gene combinations have been formed.

Immigrants from different parts of Europe have intermarried in America as they would not have done in Europe. America, in fact, is sometimes called a "melting pot" because different groups of people have been "melted" together in it. The results seem to be good.

Perhaps mankind is on the verge of another such experiment, even bigger and more extensive. Perhaps the results will be good again. Then, despite the worries we may have at present, the human race may just be beginning a new, brighter, and better stage in its history.

Index

A

A substance, 128
A_1 substance, 142
A_2 substance, 142
Aborigines, Australian, 46
   B gene frequency in, 155
   hair form of, 49
   M, N gene frequencies among, 156
   race, genetic, 158
Accents, 36
Adaptation, 121
African genetic race, 158
Africans, Rh gene frequencies among, 156, 157
Agglutination, 128, 130
   diagram of, 133
Alaska, 154
Albinos, 72, 120
Alfonso XIII, 109
Alpines, 52
Ameba, 58
   diagram of, 61
American (Indian) genetic race, 158
Americans, height of, 114
Amino acids, 67
Androgens, 115
Angles, 36
Anglo-Saxon language, 36
Anglo-Saxons, 39
Animals, classification of, 18
   blood group substances in, 152
Anti-A, 128, 130
Anti-B, 128, 130
Anti-Semitism, 38
Apes, 21, 152
Arabic language, 37, 39
Arabs, 29, 30, 39
Aramaic language, 37
Armies, interbreeding and, 29, 30
Aryan languages, 38
Aryans, 37, 38
Asia, B gene frequency in, 149, 151
Asia Minor, 38
Asian genetic race, 158
Asians, blood types of, 147
   Rh gene frequencies among, 156
Assortment, independent, 102, 103
Atom bomb, 119, 170
Atoms, 65 ff.
Australia, 39
Australian (Aboriginal) genetic race, 158
Austria, 26, 29, 31, 33
Austria-Hungary, 31, 32
Autoreproduction, 68
   imperfect, 116

B

B gene frequency (map), 150
B substance, 128
Baldness, 114
 androgens and, 115
Basque language, 158
Basques, Rh gene frequencies among, 158
Belgium, 40
Bengal, blood types in, 147
Berbers, 29
"Black race," 45 ff.
Blood, erythrocytes in, 128
 heredity and, 126 ff.
 plasma of, 128
 red cells of, 128
 of unborn child, 75
 wrong ideas about, 126
Blood donors, 127
 universal, 132
Blood-group substances, 128
 in animals, 152
Blood tests, murder and, 144
 parentage disputes and, 136 ff.
Blood transfusions, 127 ff.
 dangerous, 130
 possible (diagram), 129
Blood type A, 128
 homozygous and heterozygous, 136
 subgroups of, 142
Blood type AB, 130
 rareness of, 147
Blood type B, 128
 among Asians, 147
 homozygous and heterozygous, 136
Blood type M, 142
Blood type MN, 142
Blood type N, 142
Blood type O, 132
 among American Indians, 147
Blood types, 128 ff.
 diagram of, 131
 dominance among, 134, 135
 heterozygous, 136
 homozygous, 136
 incomplete dominance among, 135, 142
 inheritance of, 134 ff.
 races and, 145 ff.
Bones, races and, 50 ff.
Brachycephalic, 51
Breeding, selective, 20
"Brown race," 46
Bulgarian language, 34

C

Cairo, 22, 23
Canada, 39
 French-speaking people in, 33
Canidae, 19
Canis, 19
Carnivora, 19
Carotene, 43, 45
Carrots, 43

INDEX

Cat family, species among, 19
Catherine the Great, 32
Cell, 58
  diagram of, 61
  enzyme organization in, 69, 70
Cell division, 59 ff.
  diagram of, 63
Cell membrane, 61
Cells, human, chromosome number of, 62
Celtic languages, 39
Cephalic index, 51
Chance happenings, 100, 101
Characteristics, inheritance of, 95 ff.
Characteristics, linked, 103
Characteristics, national, 25 ff.
Charles XII, 27
Chemical reactions, 69
Children, inherited characteristics of, 88, 90
Chinese, height of, 50
  "national character" of, 27, 28
Chordata, 18
Chromatin, 61
Chromosome maps, 113
Chromosomes, 62 ff.
  chemical makeup of, 66 ff.
  crossing-over in, 111
  duplication of, 63 ff.
  duplication of (diagram), 68
  enzyme formation by, 70
  gene linkage and, 103
  imperfect autoreproduction of, 116
  independent assortment and, 102
  occurrence in pairs, 77 ff.
Civil War, 15
Classes, 19
Color-blindness, inheritance of, 104 ff.
  inheritance of (diagrams), 106, 107
Coptic language, 37
Cornwall, 39
Crossing of plants, 95
Crossing-over, 111
  chromosome maps and, 113
Cultural differences, 41, 42
Cyprus, 31
Cytoplasm, 60
Czech language, 32
Czechoslovakia, 31

D

Danish language, 36
Denmark, 27, 29
Diabetes, 170
Diet, head shape and, 54
  height and, 114
Differences, cultural, 41, 42
  individual, 11
  physical, 42 ff.
Discrimination, 15
Dog family, species among, 19

Dogs, selective breeding of, 20
varieties of, 21
Dolichocephalic, 51
Dominance, 89
incomplete, 99
Dominant genes, 89
Donkeys, 20
Donors, blood, 127
Dravidians, 46
Drosophila, 112
Dutch language, 34

E

Early European genetic race, 158
East African Negroes, hair of, 49
Egg cell, hen's, 74
Egg cell, human, chromosome number in, 78, 79
diagram of, 75
Egg cells, 74
development of, 74, 75
fertilization of, 76, 77
X and Y chromosomes and, 81
Egg yolk, 43
Egypt, 37, 39
appearance of population, 22, 23
Embryo, 77
England, 29
English, "national character" of, 26, 27
English language, 14, 31, 34, 36
other languages and, 36
"English-speaking peoples," 39
Environment, genes and, 113 ff.
Enzymes, 69
formation by chromosomes, 70
Epicanthic eye-fold, 49, 50
Erythrocytes, 128
Eskimos, 48, 49, 155
Ethiopian languages, 37
Eugenics, 171
European genetic race, 158
European (early) genetic race, 158
Europeans, Rh gene frequency among, 157
Evolution, 123, 124
Eye color, 49
of albinos, 72
inheritance of, 86 ff.
inheritance of (diagram), 87, 92

F

Families, 19
Females as color-blindness carriers, 107, 108
as hemophilia carriers, 109
X and Y chromosomes and, 81 ff.
Fertility, 20
Fertilization, probability and, 100, 101

Fertilized ovum, 76, 77
  chromosome number in, 79
  parents' chromosomes and, 79, 80
  sex of, 81 ff.
Feulgen reagent, 62
Finnish language, 37
Finno-Ugrian language family, 37
Foreigner, 14
Fossil remains, 124
Four o'clock, color inheritance of, 99
France, 29, 33, 40
  B gene frequency in, 149
Frederick the Great, 26
French, height of, 50
  "national character" of, 26
French language, 33, 34
  contribution to English language, 36
"French-speaking peoples," 40
Frizzy hair, 49
Fruit-fly, 112
Future, mankind and, 168 ff.

G

Gamma rays, 119
Gene frequencies, 148 ff.
  in Africa, 156
  in America, 151, 154, 156
  among the Basques, 158
  in Asia, 156
  in Australia, 151, 155, 156
  of blood group substances, 148 ff.
  of early man, 152
  in Europe, 149, 157
  and human history, 151 ff.
  in Japan, 151
  in Kharkov, 148
  in London, 148
  maps of, 149
  races determined by, 158
Gene series, 85, 101 ff.
Gene series, human, A, B, O, 132, 134
  M, N, 142, 156
  Rh, 142, 156
Gene series, pea plant, seed color, 102
  seed-form, 95 ff., 102
Genera, 19
Genes, 70 ff.
  diet and, 114
  dominant, 89
  effect on one another, 114 ff.
  enzyme formation by, 71
  imperfect autoreproduction of, 116
  independent assortment of, 102, 103
  number in human, 118
  pairs of, 85 ff.
  recessive, 89
  survival value of, 120
  variations among, 84 ff.
Genes, four o'clock, blossom color, 99

Genes, human, 85 ff.
  A, 134 ff.
  A_1, 142
  A_2, 142
  B, 134 ff.
  blond hair, 110
  blue eyes, 85 ff., 110
  brown eyes, 85 ff., 110
  brown hair, 110
  color-blindness, 104 ff.
  hemophilia, 109, 120
  M, 142
  N, 142
  O, 134 ff.
  rh, 157
  Rh^o, 156
  Rh^z, 156
Genes, pea plant, 95 ff.
  green-pea, 102
  smooth-pea, 95 ff., 102 ff.
  wrinkled-pea, 95 ff., 102 ff.
  yellow-pea, 102
Genes, undesirable, "breeding out" of, 172 ff.
Genetic drift, 152-155
Genetic races, 158
  world map of, 159
Genetics, 57
  the future and, 168 ff.
Genoa, 22
Genotypes, 91
German language, 31 ff.
  on the Volga, 32
Germanic languages, 34
Germans, "national character" of, 25, 26
Germany, 37
  B gene frequency in, 149
  national "purity" of, 29
  racism in, 16
  unification of, 30, 31
Giant, 73
Great Britain, 39
  language of, 31
Greece, 31
Greek language, 31, 38, 39
Growth hormone, 72, 73

H

Hair color, 47, 48
Hair form, races and, 48
Hair, Negro, adaptation to environment, 122
Haiti, 40
Ham, 37
Hamitic language family, 37
Head shapes, diagram of, 52
  distribution of (map), 53
  European, 52, 54
  race and, 51 ff.
  variations with diet, 54
Hebrew language, 37
Height, race and, 50
  variation with diet, 51
Hemoglobin, 43
Hemophilia, inheritance of, 109
Heredity, chance happenings and, 100, 101
"Herrenvolk," 16
Heterozygous, 86

Hitler, Adolf, 29
  nationalism of, 31
  race theories of, 37, 38
Hogs, A substance in, 152
Homo, 21
Homo sapiens, 21
Homozygous, 86
Horses, B substance in, 152
Hungarian language, 37
Hybrids, 86
Hydrogen bomb, 119, 171

I

I. Q., 165
Identifications, 12 ff.
Immigrants, Americanization of, 15, 16
Incomplete dominance, 99
Independent assortment, 102, 103
India, 38
  B gene frequency in, 51
Indians, (American), B gene frequency in, 154, 155
  blood type differences among, 154
  blood types of, 147
  genetic race, 158
  interbreeding of, 28, 29
  M, N gene frequencies among, 156
Individual differences, 11
Indo-Dravidian genetic race, 160
Indo-European language family, 34, 38

"Inferior races," 16, 17, 165 ff.
Inheritance, blood-type, 134 ff.
  color-blindness, 104 ff.
  eye-color, 86 ff.
  hemophilia, 109
  intelligence, 162 ff.
  rules of, 95 ff.
  sex-linked, 104 ff.
  sex-linked (tables), 106, 107
Intelligence, inheritance of, 162 ff.
Intelligence quotient (I.Q.), 164
Intelligence tests, 164
  value of, 165 ff.
Interbreeding among peoples, 28 ff.
Iran, B gene frequency in, 151
Ireland, 30, 39
Isogenes, 149
Italian language, 31, 34
Italy, 22
  unification of, 31

J

Japan, 30
  A gene frequency in, 151
Japanese, 49
  height of, 50
  "national character" of, 27, 28
Java Man, 124

Jews, language of, 38
  Nazi view of, 16, 17, 38
Jutes, 36

K

Kharkov, gene frequencies in, 148
Kingdoms, 18
Kinky hair, 48, 49

L

Languages, 30 ff.
  Anglo-Saxon, 36
  Arabic, 37, 39
  Aramaic, 37
  Aryan, 38
  Basque, 158
  Bulgarian, 34
  Celtic, 39
  Coptic, 37
  Czech, 32
  Danish, 36
  Dutch, 34
  English, 14, 31, 34, 36
  Ethiopian, 37
  European (map of), 35
  families of, 33 ff.
  French, 33, 34, 36
  Finno-Ugrian, 37
  German, 31 ff.
  Germanic, 34
  Greek, 31, 38, 39
  Hamitic, 37
  Hebrew, 37
  Hungarian, 37
  Indo-European, 34, 38
  Italian, 31, 34
  Latin, 34
  Persian, 34
  Polish, 32, 34
  Portuguese, 34
  race and, 32 ff.
  Romance, 34
  Rumanian, 32, 34
  Russian, 34
  Sanskrit, 34
  Semitic, 37
  Serbian, 32, 34
  Slavic, 34
  Spanish, 34
  Swedish, 34
  Turkish, 37, 39
  Yiddish, 38
Latin America, interbreeding in, 28
Latin language, 34
  contribution to English language, 36
Lemurs, 21
Liberia, 39, 40
Libya, 39
Linked characteristics, 103
Liver cell, diagram of, 61
London, gene frequencies in, 148
Louisiana, 40
  French-speaking people in, 33

M

M substance, 142

Males, color-blindness among, 108
  hemophilia among, 109
  as weaker sex, 82, 84
  X and Y chromosomes of, 81 ff.
Mammalia, 19
Man, blood types of, 128 ff.
  evolution of, 124
  future of, 168 ff.
  genetic races of, 158, 159
  possible deterioration of, 169, 170
Manchuria, B gene frequency in, 151
"Master race," 16
Maturation, 78
Mediterraneans, 54
Melanin, 43, 45
  in eyes, 49
  formation from tyrosine, 71, 72
  in hair, 47
Mendel, Gregor Johann, 95 ff.
Mendel's Laws, 97
Mesocephalic, 52
Mestizos, 28, 29
Metaphase, 63
Metazoa, 59
Mexico, 28
Midget, 73
Minority, 15
Mitochondria, 69
Mitosis, 63
Modena, 31
Mohammedanism, 29

Molecules, 65 ff.
Mongols, 49
Monkeys, 19, 21, 152
Monroe, James, 40
Monrovia, 40
Moors, 29
Mulattoes, 24
Mules, 20
Mummies, 144
Muscle cells, 59
  diagram of, 61
Mutation, 116 ff.
  atomic explosions and, 119, 170
  beneficial, 120 ff.
  diagram of, 117
  frequency of, 118
  future, 170, 171
  harmful, 118 ff.
  hit-or-miss, 123
  X-rays and, 119, 170

N

N substance, 142
Naples, 31
Napoleon, 26
National characteristics, 25 ff.
National "purity," 28 ff.
National Socialists, 16
Nationalism, 31 ff.
  among non-Europeans, 31 n.
  war and, 31
Natural selection, 122

Nazis, 16
Neanderthal Man, 124
Negroes, 46
 adaptation to environment, 122
 differences from white men, 22 ff.
 English-speaking, 39, 40
 French-speaking, 40
 hair form of, 48, 49
 height of, 50
 in Latin America, 28
 prejudice against, 15
 skin color of, 43
 in the United States, 24
 variations in color of, 46
"Negro blood," 126, 127
Nerve cells, 59
 diagram of, 61
New Guinea, 48
Nicholas II, 109
Nile river, 23
Noah, 37
Non-Aryans, 38
Nordics, 52
Normans, 36
North Africa, 29, 39
Nose, adaptation to environment, 122
Nuclear membrane, 60, 63
Nucleoprotein, in chromosomes, 66 ff.
 in mitochondria, 69, 70
Nucleus, cell, 60

O

Orders, 19

Ovaries, 76
Ovum, 74
 fertilized, 76, 77
Ovum, human, 76

P

Pan-Germanism, 37
Pan-Slavism, 37
Parentage disputes, 136 ff.
Parentage, possible and impossible (diagrams), 137, 139, 141
Parma, 31
Pea plants, 95 ff.
Peking Man, 124
Pennsylvania "Dutch," 33
Pentoses, 67
Persian language, 34
Phenotypes, 91
 1-2-1 ratio of, 99
 3-1 ratio of, 97 ff.
 16-9-3-3-1 ratio of, 103
Philippine Islands, 40
Phosphate ions, 67
Phylum, 18
Physical characteristics, inheritance of, 95 ff.
Physical differences, 42 ff.
Pigments, skin, 43, 45
Pistil, 95
Pituitary gland, 72
Placenta, 75
Plasma, 128
 transfusion of, 132
Poland, 31
 Nazi view of, 16
 partitions of, 33

Polish language, 32, 34
Pollen, 95
Portuguese language, 34
Prejudice, 15
Primates, 21
Probability, 99-101
Protoplasm, 58
Protozoa, 58
Prussia, 26, 31, 33
Pure lines, 86
Purines, 67
"Purity," national, 28 ff.
Pygmies, 50
Pyrenees mountains, 158
Pyrimidines, 67

Q

Quebec, 40
    French-speaking people in, 33

R

Race, 12
    "alpine," 52
    "aryan," 37, 38
    "black," 45
    blood types and, 145 ff.
    "brown," 46
    gene frequencies and, 158
    genetic, 158 ff.
    hair form and, 48
    head shape and, 51 ff.
    height and, 50
    "inferior," 16, 17, 165 ff.
    languages and, 32 ff.
    "Mediterranean," 54
    "non-Aryan," 38
    "Nordic," 52
    physical differences and, 42 ff.
    "red," 46
    skin color and, 43 ff.
    "superior," 16, 17, 165 ff.
    usefulness of notion to scientists, 56
    "white," 45
    within species, 21
    "yellow," 45
    "yellow-brown," 46
Racism, 15-18, 37, 162 ff.
    final statement on, 167, 168
Reactions, chemical, 69
Recessive genes, 89
    reappearance of, 91, 98
Red cells, 128
"Red race," 46
Rh gene series, inheritance of, 156, 157
Rh-negative, 156 ff.
Rh-positive, 156 ff.
Rh substance, 143
rh substance, 156
Rh^o substance, 156
Rh^z substance, 156
Rhesus monkey, 143
Rhodesian Man, 124
Rickets, 54
Romance languages, 34
Rumanian language, 32, 34

Russia, 26, 29, 33, 37
  B gene frequency in, 149
  German-speaking people in, 32
  Nazi view of, 16
Russian language, 34
Russians, "national character" of, 27

S

Sanskrit language, 34
Sardinia, 31
Saxons, 36
Scandinavians, 50
Seed, 95
Selection, natural, 122
Selective breeding, 20
Semen, 76
Semitic language family, 37
Serbian language, 32, 34
Serum, 143
Sex determination, 81, 82
  diagram of, 83
Sex-linked inheritance, 104 ff.
  diagrams of, 106, 107
Shem, 37
Sicily, 22, 50
Skeletons, 18
Skin cells, 59
Skin color, change through tanning, 47
  distribution of (map), 44
  pigments and, 43, 45
  race and, 43 ff.
  usefulness of, 121

"Slant eyes," 49
Slavic languages, 34
Solomon, 136
South Africa, 39
Southern states, Negroes in, 24
Spain, 29, 30
  B gene frequency in, 149
Spanish language, 34
Species, 19
  definition of, 20
  race and, 21
Sperm cells, 76
  chromosome number in human, 78, 79
  diagram of, 75
  X and Y chromosomes and, 82
Spermatozoa, 76
Straight hair, 48, 49
Sudan, 24
"Superior races," 16, 17, 165 ff.
Survival value, 120
Sweden, 29
Swedes, "national character" of, 27
Swedish language, 34
Swiss, "national character" of, 27
Switzerland, 40

T

Taxonomy, 18
Testes, 76

INDEX

Turkish language, 37, 39
Tuscany, 31
Tyrosinase, 72
Tyrosine, 71

U

United Nations, 17
United States, 17, 30, 39
   accents in, 36
   American Indians in, 28
   French-speaking people in, 33
   language of, 31
   Negroes of, 24
Universal donor, 132

V

Victoria, 109, 115
Vitamin D, 54
Volga River, 32

W

Wales, 39

War, nationalism and, 31
   racism and, 17
Wavy hair, 48, 49
White men, differences from Negroes, 22 ff.
   melanin in the skin of, 43
"White race," 45 ff.
Whole blood, 132
World War I, 25, 32, 33
World War II, 17, 25, 32

X

X-chromosome, 81 ff.
   sex linkage and, 104 ff.
X-rays, mutations and, 119, 170

Y

Y-chromosome, 81 ff.
   sex linkage and, 104 ff.
"Yellow race," 45
"Yellow-brown race," 46
Yiddish language, 38